Come

W. L. Lloyd-Jones (Buster to his countless friends) was, until illness incapacitated him a few years ago, known to thousands of animal lovers as possibly the most skilful veterinary practitioner ever to have practised his art.

In this sequel to his immensely successful first book, *The Animals Came In One By One*, he describes how he overcame his handicap, despite being given only a year to live. Once again his writing abounds in delightful anecdotes, concerning the rich and famous as well as his animal friends.

Come Into My World

Buster Lloyd-Jones

Illustrated by Stella Mackie

Fontana/Collins

First published by Martin Secker & Warburg Ltd. 1972
First issued in Fontana Books 1973

Copyright © W. L. Lloyd-Jones 1972

Printed in Great Britain
Collins Clear-Type Press
London and Glasgow

Buster Lloyd-Jones is most grateful to Stella Mackie
for the gift of the drawings illustrating this book

The cover picture appears by courtesy
of Spectrum Colour Library

Contents

To Dorothy
for her devotion and kindness
over the trying years

Also to the Doctors, Nurses and Physiotherapists,
particularly on Floor Four,
at King Edward VII Hospital, Midhurst

Chapter One

RESIGNATION AND SUCCESS

The weather matched my mood when I wrote that fateful letter. Although it was high summer – 25 June 1965, I will never forget the date – it was a dark and forbidding afternoon. A fierce south-westerly gale pounded the shingle on Hove beach and the spray reached high to the windows of The Penthouse as I laboriously scrawled my signature on the letter that would change my life. It was addressed to the Royal Veterinary College asking them to take me off the register of practising vets. My ailing body had let me down again, and I felt as though I was signing away my life.

When I look back over my years, I cannot remember a time when I felt more hopeless. I had recently left hospital and the doctors had given me a year to live. I was in constant pain, and the attack of polio which had crippled my body and confined me to a wheelchair had also affected my lungs. I was a physical wreck. Had I been a dog it would have been kinder, I thought, to have me put to sleep. And now, to add to all my troubles, I had just terminated my only source of income. The spectre of poverty lined up with all my other adversaries and it made a frightening and formidable display. My mood matched the day.

There was only one glimmer of hope. My book *The Animals Came In One By One* was soon to be published by Secker & Warburg, and I knew they expected great things from it. But I was not so confident. I could not, in all honesty, see people paying good money to read my disconnected ramblings about animals. And yet . . .?

Little did I know that my life was soon to take another bewildering turn. And, as in so many times in the past, the animals were the key.

As publication day approached, I worked myself up into a frenzy of doubt. Would anyone read the book? Would the reviewers tear it to pieces before it reached the shops? Or, worse, would they not bother to review it at all? I became so frightened at one stage that I tried to kill the book on my own initiative. I rang the publishers, and asked them to stop publication. They said it wasn't possible, because many thousands had already been printed. And would I please stop fussing? But it really didn't help. I rang again and asked how much it would cost for me to buy the lot. I would rather have burned them myself than risk the scorn of the literary world. There is no doubt like self-doubt.

I am not a superstitious man, but I did not consider the omens had been favourable. Apart from the agony of ripping sixty thousand words out of oneself and setting them down on paper, I had had trouble with the illustrations.

I didn't *quite* know what I wanted, but I knew just what I didn't want. And I didn't really want many of the sketches presented by the artist. But time was running short and finally I had to approve them. There was nothing technically wrong with them, you understand – many people have been complimentary about them – but I did not feel they fitted. But I drew the line at the sketch of me on the cover. It didn't even look like me. Instead of my homely time-worn features, there was a blond hard-faced stranger who would not have looked out of place on a Wehrmacht recruiting poster. He looked confident and fit, and I was neither. So I stopped the cover; which was all very well, but it still hadn't solved the problem of the picture. I had always wanted Ronald Searle to illustrate the book, because I admire his work tremendously and his dachshund is a very good friend of mine. But Ronald was abroad, and so was his dachs, so there was no help from that quarter. Suddenly I had a brainwave. I remembered that my friend Stella Cox, the artist who paints as Stella Mackie, had painted a portrait of me. I hadn't seen it, but I knew if Stella had done it it would be good. I phoned her sister – Stella was then in Canada and would be for some time. When I explained my predicament, her sister used some of the family initiative and broke into the studio. She gave me the picture, which I thought was superb, and this subsequently appeared on the book.

There was an amusing sequel to all this. When Stella heard the news she wailed: 'But I hadn't finished it. I hadn't truly conveyed the villainy of Buster's impression. And I hadn't signed it properly.'

I had the second fright just two days before publication. I was terribly distressed at the time, because the incident looked like losing me a good friend.

The big day was the Monday. There was a publication party arranged for the Sunday evening at The Penthouse, when the reviews in the Sunday papers would give some indication of how the book had been received. There were cases of champagne on hand, and I was prepared to celebrate or drown my sorrows, whichever was the order of the day.

On the Saturday, the day before the party, I was driven over to see some friends at Goring-by-Sea. I felt I had to get away from the grisly pre-party preparations which might so easily become a wake rather than a celebration. And, on my way back, I saw a huge placard outside a newsagent's shop. It said, in letters that seemed a mile high, 'Local Vet Tells All'. I was wrapped in desperation when I read the appropriate news item. It was a full-page review of the book in my local paper, the Brighton *Evening Argus*. And it was most laudatory.

What was wrong with that? Two things: the *Argus* had jumped the gun and the publisher's embargo. It is traditional that the national Sunday newspapers get the first chance to review books to be published on a Monday. Secondly, I had promised my good friend Collie Knox, the famous columnist, first crack in the *Argus*. I had promised Collie this in all good faith, and he had received his review copy two weeks earlier, but so, of course, had the local newspaper. The difference was that Collie honoured the embargo and the *Argus* didn't. To make matters worse, Collie had already written a piece on the book, and intended to use it in his regular *Argus column* on the Tuesday. In the words of the newspaperman, Collie had been 'scooped' – and by his own newspaper at that! On top of that, he had to conjure up another item for his column because he refused to print anything which had previously appeared.

The poor chap was hopping mad and he wrote me an angry letter. I felt very bad about the whole thing and, although it was not my fault, I wrote back begging his pardon. Later he wrote a piece in his inimitable style in his column recommending the book.

That Saturday night I was quietly desperate and had no sleep at all. And the following morning I had to contain myself until 10 am because rail trouble had delayed the Sunday papers on their way from London. When I did get them they were almost ripped to shreds in my eagerness to search them. I couldn't believe my eyes when I read the reviews. To a man, the reviewers praised the book to the heavens. It was hailed as a 'masterpiece', 'a must for animal lovers the world over', and similar, vastly encouraging phrases. I was dazed, but still worried. Would people buy it? It was money I needed more than praise.

But for all that, it was a splendid party. It started at six o'clock and finished at eleven, and it seemed to me there was more liquid flowing in The Penthouse than in the sea outside. Considerably stronger, too. It was my first literary thrash – and far from my last – and I was grateful that it was fought out on my home ground.

The following morning the book's success was established even to my satisfaction. The publisher was taken by surprise. Harrods, for instance, were selling copies so quickly that they had to send taxis down to the distributors to fill up again. Gradually, it began to dawn on me that I might have a bestseller on my hands.

To my mind, the event which confirmed success was when the *Liverpool Post* asked to serialise the book. I had always considered Liverpool to be one of the farthest-flung outposts of the Commonwealth, and the knowledge that the city's own newspaper thought enough of my book to want to serialise it was the ultimate reassurance. Following closely behind came another pleasant surprise: the *News of the World* wanted the serial too! In fact, so many newspapers and magazines did serialise it, or at least printed huge extracts, that I then became worried that no one would have need actually to buy the book! But that was nonsense, of course, and the extra publicity played a major part in the book's success.

I met so many journalists I lost count. But one newspaperman I really felt sorry for was Jack Curtis from the

Reveille. He spent the whole of one day taking hundreds of photographs from all angles. I was getting double vision from all the attacks of his flash gun by the time he left. But when the series appeared, the magazine didn't use one single photograph, just drawings from an artist who had never seen me.

It was all very gratifying becoming known overnight, but the publicity from press, radio and television had one big drawback. I had so many letters from people thanking me for writing the book, and telling me their troubles, and the troubles of their pets, that I had to employ two secretaries to help me with the replies. I have had more than 8,000 letters inspired by the book to date. I feel bound to answer them all, and it has cost me a small fortune in stamps. Some of the letters are incredible. People even tell me about their personal life, and some of the revelations are astonishing. The Americans seem particularly frank in this department. They must think I'm a Dr Kinsey, and not just a poor old ex-vet.

I have a formula for answering these letters. I simply write back and tell them that a man like myself is really in no position to give advice on these very delicate matters!

Success shimmered round me in delicious waves. A genuine Indian Maharanee – a gorgeous creature in a sari and dripping with jewels – came down to see me. She was an expert on tropical birds and had a famous collection back home in India, along with a zoo-full of animals. She asked me to go out to Delhi and supervise them. The amount of money she mentioned made my head whirl, but reluctantly I had to decline. I really didn't feel up to a trip to India, and then having to cope with the heat *and* half a dozen Bengal tigers. Besides, I know very little about birds.

One thing I did find was that I attended more parties. These varied in presentation but all had one thing in common: when one is confined to a wheelchair, one constitutes virtually a captive audience. The party bore seems to home on me with the accuracy of a guided missile – and there are few parties without at least one bore.

One party I shall never forget was thrown by Hatchard's bookshop, and it was packed with *real* authors, like Nicholas

Monsarrat, A. P. Herbert, and my old friend, Denise Robins. Denise was absolutely marvellous at this particular party. She was used to it of course, while I felt completely out of my depth, and she obviously sensed that I was somewhat over-awed by the glittering celebrities, many of whom had written lots of best-sellers. Denise was then writing her 150th novel.

At one point of the evening I was nervously chatting to Harold Macmillan about politics, of all things, when Denise sensed I was in some difficulty and sailed in to the rescue. She had a Yorkshire terrier called Buttons who had weak hindquarters caused by a misplaced hip.

'Buster,' said Denise sweetly, 'what *are* we going to do about Buttons' bottom?'

If the former prime minister was surprised, he certainly did not show it. He just looked inscrutable, which is, I suppose, a necessity for poker players and politicians. But he did ask me the best way to train a gun-shy sporting dog. I suggested that he should get some herbal nerve pills to build up the dog's confidence and feed the nervous system.

I have never been a hard-drinking man – these days I mustn't drink at all – but I must confess that I got slightly high that night. I think I was tacking round the room in my wheelchair and it was a good job I wasn't breathalysed.

After the party I adjourned to Robert Carrier's restaurant and had a wonderful meal. This was by way of being a re-union, because Bob and I were great friends. In fact, I was once his boss! I first met him many years ago in Paris and we got on splendidly. Bob was depressed about certain domestic problems and felt he needed a change. The upshot was that I invited him over to London to run Denes Veter-inary Herbal Products. Bob ran Denes very well. But he always does things on the grand scale – his books are bigger than anyone else's – and he used to order materials for the company on the grand scale too. We always managed to pay the bills, but he caused us plenty of frights. He also used vast quantities of eggs, butter and stuff when he kept his culinary hand in at Denes Close, my animal hospital in Preston Park, Brighton. He never could understand our rationing system, and would use up a whole week's ration on one meal with gay abandon. But I must say it was well worth while when one ate the result.

After dinner in his restaurant, I went back to Bob's lovely house in Islington, where I was promptly asked to treat Hoover, his pug, for what turned out to be a stomach upset. I told Bob the dog was eating too much of his master's cooking! And that's not right for any dog, however *haute cuisine* his master may be.

They were happy, hectic days, but nothing to what was ahead. Things really started to pop when John Day, the big American publishers, invited me over to New York to launch an American edition of my book. Phone calls were made backwards and forwards over the Atlantic at vast expense, and I was delighted when Days booked me a suite at my favourite hotel, the Westbury in Madison Avenue. But trust me to worry about something. As I left Southampton on board the *United States*, I began to wonder whether I could physically stand the strain of America's renowned hospitality.

I became so steamed up about it that when we docked at Cherbourg before crossing the 'herring pond', I rang Dorothy Pearson at home just to hear a friendly and familiar voice. Dorothy asked me if I had made any friends and I told her: 'No, everyone's hanging over the rail goggling at the Duke and Duchess of Windsor who are coming on board.' Trust Dorothy to get everything back to normal. I nearly fainted when she said: 'Do remember me to them,' and then I recalled she knew them both quite well: Dorothy had been the women's golf champion of Great Britain and had played with them both at Sunningdale.

I had the opportunity to pass on Dorothy's message sooner than I thought. The second day out they invited me to drinks in their stateroom and complimented me on the book, although they had previously written to say how much they enjoyed it. Actually, I had met them briefly some years before – once at a dog show in Paris, and once at a party in Marbella on the Costa del Sol. We had a convivial little session, and I was called on to inspect and admire their two pugs, both of whom were below par – probably a little sea-sick. We said goodbye and arranged to meet again after dinner.

In fact, we met again during dinner, and there was quite a

little furore too. One of the cabaret artists had rather a clever trick in which he pulled six doves out of walking sticks and things. He did this two at a time, and the doves were trained to fly off briefly and then return to his assistant's hand. However, that night there was a gale blowing – it became worse as the voyage continued – and even that great ship was rolling and pitching. I had to keep a wary eye out for my wheelchair which was in danger of wallowing around like loose ballast. I found the crook of a walking stick very handy for anchoring myself on to things.

The movement of the ship created problems for the act. Then two doves flew up into the dome in the roof and became entangled in some electric-light cables. The Duchess was most upset. 'Buster, please *do* something,' she said. It was practically a royal command, but what I was to do I just could not imagine. I would dearly have loved to leap out of my wheelchair and swarm up the chandeliers to the rescue, but it just wasn't on.

I did manage to call a steward who found a ladder and somewhat perilously climbed up and untangled the birds. He got the loudest cheers of the evening and the Duchess called him over personally and thanked him. I looked at the birds, but apart from being frightened they were quite unhurt.

This incident made me realise just how fond of birds and animals she is. I know that since she went to live in France she has become patron or president of many animal societies, and that she does a marvellous job. Unhappily, not all animals are treated well, and quite often the Duchess puts on a head scarf and dark glasses and sallies forth to the rescue of dogs and cats she knows are being ill-treated.

After dinner we continued our conversation which I found most interesting. I find them very with-it and young in heart and up to date in their ways of thinking. I thoroughly enjoyed the evening, which leads me to ask, although I do not want to revive an ancient controversy, why can't the Duke and Duchess of Windsor come back and live out their remaining years in England? Is protocol so strict? It is so sad to think of them wandering and banished to the end of their lives. 1936 was a long time ago, and I would have thought by now they had expiated their 'wrong' in loving each other.

That was a terribly rough trip. Apparently only a few passengers survived it without being seasick, and I was one of them. I must admit it gave me quite a feeling of superiority to lurch down in my wheelchair and eat a hearty meal in a dining-room practically devoid of passengers.

When a man gets above himself, I would heartily recommend a sea trip in a force ten storm to give him an injection of humility. Even in a modern liner, the fury of the elements reaches out and shows him he's not such a big chap after all.

There was one incident which chilled everybody, including the crew. There was thick fog as well as a huge sea on the Sunday, and an unusual number of people attended the church service. When Matins were over they reeled out of church to the bar – a most unusual sequence of events – then, suddenly, there was a tremendous gasp. Looming out of the fog, only a mile or so away, was a huge iceberg. It was an eerie and menacing sight which chilled us all. I am sure I was not the only passenger thinking about the *Titanic* and trying to remember how many tenths of an iceberg were hidden under the water. The ship changed course and slowed down for a while, and I thought again how nature can put us back in our place. I spoke to the captain at dinner that night and he told me there had been no danger – the iceberg had shown up on his radar, but it was most unusual to see one so far south at that time of the year.

We finally docked twenty hours late with numerous bruises among passengers and crew and broken crockery littering the sea bed in our wake. It must have been the sea air, but I felt marvellous, ready for a ten-rounder in Madison Square Garden any day!

On the run-in to New York, however, I gazed at the fantastic skyline and began to lose some of my bounce. I knew that American hospitality and business methods matched the size of its architecture and I began again to wonder what I had let myself in for.

We docked – I was soon to find out.

Chapter Two

THE AMERICAN ROUND-ABOUT

When I look back on my American tour, it seems like a dream. I often think I haven't really lived life to the full since I returned. It was three weeks of happy confusion, highlighted by memorable characters and events I shall never forget. The ballyhoo started the moment the *United States'* gangway touched the pier. I peered timidly over the rail, muffled in plaid rugs, and what I saw almost made me trundle away to the bilges to hide. I saw an army of what were quite obviously journalists, with batteries of cameramen and television cameras, all milling ferociously about, bent on scooping everyone else. They plunged up the gangplank like latterday pirates, with press cards instead of knives clenched between their teeth, bowed down with the weight of all the paraphernalia of modern mass media.

I thought: 'Good grief, the circus has started already,' but to my great relief they dashed past me, feet churning with eagerness, faces drawn with anxiety in case they missed anything, and crashed in a blaze of flash guns into the stateroom of the Windsors, who were holding a press conference.

I was thinking, God bless the Duke and Duchess for turning aside the hordes, when a steward fetched me for an urgent phone call. It was from the New York publishers and they sternly forbade me to give any interviews until I was told. 'No premature exposure,' the voice said, 'we gotta get organised because the delay has upset the schedule. Sit tight and we'll send someone for you.' I felt just like a steak and kidney pie, or a packet of detergent, or some other new product waiting to be launched.

The 'someone' was Eileen Lottman, a publicity executive with John Day, who was to wheel me and deal me into a frenetic round of activity, all designed, of course, to sell copies of my book. It's a good job I kept that point firmly in mind, because sometimes I felt we were on opposing sides.

Eileen was a tiny woman, terribly kind and efficient, but

very badly dressed. I had spoken to her often on the phone and formed quite a different image. I had quite expected her to look like something out of Harper's Bazaar. By sheer force of personality Eileen whisked me through customs and into a huge, centrally heated limousine, with a cocktail bar and hot and cold running trimmings. The driver of the car was called Benny, a tall thin, coloured man who looked like a stick of liquorice and turned out to be my constant companion and an immortal character.

On the way from ship to hotel, Eileen gave me an itinerary – she called it a 'skedule' – and a formidable document it was. It was like three pieces of foolscap end to end and it proved quite conclusively that my free time was going to be numbered in minutes. And because the ship had been twenty hours late, the programme was cramped still further. I booked in at the hotel and didn't even have time to wash. Benny, who had immediately and miraculously acquired the knack of loading me from car to wheelchair, whisked me straight round to a recording studio for a radio broadcast.

An executive met me at the door, and just as we were going in he said: 'If you're feeling homesick, Mr Lloyd-Jones, take a look over there.' I looked, and saw none other than Lord Snowdon, bearded and casually dressed, getting into a car. Apparently he was over on some photographic business and, because Princess Margaret wasn't with him, the New York papers had built it up into a scandal. I'm told there's *always* a scandal in New York, and if the papers can't find one they will make one.

I thought it a strange business, this recording. The interview lasted for nearly three hours, and the show was called 'Good Living, Lorraine'. As it was a commercial, they asked me to say 'Good living, Lorraine', every time they indicated. They wanted, of course, a good, rich, pukka British accent, but I found to my horror that every time I recited the magic phrase, my accent lapsed into a caricature of rough Brooklynese. They gave me a record afterwards, and to this day I squirm with embarrassment when I hear my voice rasping 'Good livin', Lorraine' like a bit player in a Damon Runyon-inspired movie.

Although I didn't realise it then, this first day was comparatively relaxed. Benny took me back to the hotel for a rest, and he drove that enormous Cadillac like a destroyer, berthing it into slots in the traffic at the lights, then surging forward again as though the devil was after us. He was engaged in a battle of long standing with the New York cabbies – no angels themselves – and he showed no quarter. Actually, he drove like I used to do, and I thoroughly enjoyed the experience.

That night, after a much-needed rest, John Day himself and his exquisite Chinese wife took me out to dinner at the Pavilion, one of the best restaurants in New York. It was a huge place and had a beautiful décor in pale blue, lit by enormous crystal chandeliers, a most appropriate setting for the gorgeous Mrs Day, who was like a tiny, exotic bird. Sometimes her cheongsam fell open, revealing a stretch of leg that would have made Aphrodite sulk with envy. Even this turned out to be a working dinner. Corps of pressmen approached in line astern, all asking the same questions and, apparently, taking the same photographs.

For most of the trip I was engaged in a running fight with the photographers. I didn't mind having my picture taken, but I was determined not to be shown in my wheelchair. I developed some tactics to prevent this, looking away, ostensibly scratching my head, or burying my face in a magazine or newspaper. When great haste was required, I evolved a frightening grimace that must have looked as though I was having a heart attack. But I couldn't win all the time. One photographer got me with a most astonishing expression on my face, and his newspaper used the picture

with a caption which implied that I was drunk! Or 'on the sauce' as they term it.

The following day brought an amazing experience of the type that could only happen in America. I was returning to my hotel for a photographic session involving animals. As we started towards the lobby, which was just like the entrance to Claridges, I saw, of all things, a man walking an ocelot on a lead. Honestly!

As they drew level, the ocelot jumped straight into my lap. It was a beautiful animal, although rather nervous, I thought. We disengaged, the owner apologised, and we went on in to see Eileen, who was waiting for the animals to arrive with all the nervousness of her profession. I told her about the ocelot, and she shot off like a bullet, returning with the ocelot and its escort. She muttered something about 'exploiting windfall opportunities', and back on my lap went the cat, while the photographers practically stood on their heads taking pictures.

It transpired that the animal belonged to none other than Salvador Dali, and the man with the lead was his secretary. Salvador has never exactly shunned publicity, and he rang the publishers when all the pictures appeared in the press, saying why on earth wasn't he sent for? After all, that was why he kept the creature!

One thing struck me as being both bizarre and tragic. The pictures were taken in the hotel lobby while all the hotel guests were taking tea. They think this is very British, poor things, whereas American tea tastes exactly like British coffee. It seemed that every other woman was wearing either a leopard or an ocelot coat. If I had been that animal, I would have felt very nervous. It was quite an anti-climax when the other animals arrived. There was a chimp, and a few dogs – including one beautiful curly-coated retriever – but none of them carried anything like the impact of the ocelot.

As the television appearances continued, it seemed to me that the rivalling producers were trying to outdo each other with the animals I was to appear with. I was photographed festooned with snakes, with bush babies, a bear cub, a lion cub, and even an alligator. I often felt very sorry for these reluctant stars. Most of them were frightened to death by the noise and the bustle – I know I was – and disturbed by the heat and glare from the arc lights. Once, I refused to appear with a lion cub dressed up in pink satin because it was clearly scared out of its wits. I much preferred radio, because there were no lights, but there were no animals either, as the visual effects were lacking.

The Americans are great organisers, and my schedule was a miracle of timing with everything dovetailing into position with the accuracy of a Chippendale chair. There was only one organisational mistake in the entire tour. This occurred at the famous Algonquin Hotel, where I had an appointment with Casper Citron, a famous radio celebrity, in his studio suite. I arrived twenty minutes before the appointed time, and found everyone in a panic. They had given me the wrong time and the show was due to begin. At that stage, I didn't even know it was a show. But it was, and a live one at that.

I prepared in world-record time and found myself in a forty-five minute show compèred by Casper, alongside the deputy mayor of New York, who smelled strongly of after-shave lotion, and a large coloured woman. We embarked on a series of chats, and I was asked for my humble opinions on the expressed views of my fellow guests. As these included items like the crime rate of New York and the question of civil rights in deepest Georgia, you will appreciate I was at something of a disadvantage. I know nothing about New York crime, except that it is considerable, and all I know about the deep south would fit into a mint julep glass. So I ad-libbed furiously. Strangely enough, everyone thought I had done splendidly. But I would have been grateful to receive forewarning. A little intelligent preparation goes a long way towards concealing profound ignorance.

I had one particularly incredible experience with radio. I was due to appear in the 'Peter Lind Hayes and Mary Healey Show', a live breakfast show compèred by the couple, who are husband and wife. It was to be broadcast from their glorious house in Connecticut, about two hours' drive from New York. I found that lots of personalities operated from home, incidentally. Perhaps they got vast income tax relief from it.

Dear old Benny, as accurate as a chronometer as usual, called for me at the crack of dawn and we drove over the snow-packed roads on a bitterly cold day. As Benny picked me up, he commented: 'Jeez, boss, you don't weigh nuttin,' and in the car he insisted I ate a huge sandwich, which was certainly his breakfast. I knew that he would be offended if I refused, so I very carefully ditched the massive sandwich en route. I hope a car didn't hit it – it was big enough to cause an accident.

I arrived on time and, after introductions to my charming hosts we got settled round the breakfast table in a basement room that also served as the studio. Suddenly, water started gushing in – apparently a huge section of water pipe had fractured. It rose at a fearful rate, but in the best traditions of show business, it was decided that the show must go on. I was all right. Because of my polio I can quite comfortably sit on my crossed legs in a very fair imitation of the Lotus Position in Yoga. It's not so much a question of muscle control as having no muscles to control. So there I sat, my lower half hidden by the tablecloth, while Peter and Mary sat, eating and chatting lightly, with water surging through the room halfway to their knees.

The most amusing thing about this astonishing episode was the sight of the couple's coloured cook, sloshing around, serving food and 'cawfee' with a deep southern accent, just as though nothing unusual was happening. On her feet she wore rubber boots that looked like a cross between Wellingtons and waders. And instead of lifting her feet as she walked, she shuffled along with a skiing motion, kicking up a healthy bow-wave. I have often wondered what the listeners made of the sloshing noises in the background – or perhaps they were edited out.

On the way back from one interview, I had money trouble for the first time since the book came out. And it was all Benny's fault. I happened to remark to Benny that I didn't think much of this tour, because I hadn't even had time to go shopping for a few clothes. I will never forget the look on Benny's face. He half turned in the driver's seat and rolled up his eyes in an agony of remorse.

'You shadda told me before, boss,' he exclaimed. Three minutes later he shrieked to a halt outside Saks in the middle of Fifth Avenue, treating the parking laws with massive contempt.

'We'll be OK here, boss, because everybody in Noo York knows you by now. You're a big wheel in this town,' he said, plonking me into my wheelchair.

He pushed me right into Saks, and in no time at all I was trying suits on like mad. One was beautiful – real cashmere, and the jacket (which is all I bother about, in a sartorial sense, of course) fitted me as though it had been tailored in Savile Row. The only alterations needed were slight modifications to the backs of the jackets. These were done immediately and the finished garments were delivered to my hotel within three hours. Imagine that happening in England!

Benny insisted on acting as the go-between with me and the salesman. I asked Benny what the suit cost, he consulted the salesman, screwed up his face with anguish as he converted dollars into sterling, and told me, 'About £20, boss.' I couldn't believe my ears. But I didn't have to carry money and I knew nothing about New York prices, so I promptly ordered three suits, a few odds and ends, and a dashing trilby hat. The bill was to be sent round to the hotel, and off we went. When the bill did arrive, I nearly passed out. Benny's mental arithmetic was not up to his driving, and his costings were way out. The bill was more than £200, and the hat alone cost £18!

The following day was, as the Americans say, the big one. I was due to appear on a television show called 'Today'. It had the largest viewing audience of any show in the world – people from the States and Canada watched it religiously. When I arrived at the studio I was made up and given a bagel (Jewish bread) and coffee. I was fearfully nervous when I thought that something like one and a half times the population of England was going to see me. However, I had a mental boost from a most unexpected quarter. I was due on immediately after an interview with Bobby Kennedy. And I saw Bobby staggering out after fluffing his lines dreadfully. I felt very sorry for him. Is there anything more pathetic than a career politician getting into a muddle in front of millions of potential voters? It gave me great heart. Surely no one would expect me to be better than Bobby Kennedy, and I thanked God I wasn't following a polished, impeccable performance.

Just before the cameras started whirring, Hugh Downs, the interviewer, asked me if I was nervous. I gulped and nodded. He asked me if I doodled and would it help? I nodded again, and he gave me a pen and note pad.

The audience comprised an army of electricians and technicians, and I was doodling like fury during the interview. It really did help. Suddenly I saw on a monitor set a pair of hands drawing little blobs. Mine, it turned out. On American television, not even doodles are sacred. I have often wondered what would have happened if I had been drawing naked ladies or something! As a matter of fact, all my doodling takes the form of square hats, square faces and square men – all very Freudian and indicating, perhaps, that I am an old square. Later, a newspaper published a character analysis of me based on my doodling. I hate to record that they weren't very far out, either.

As it happened, the show was a great success. The Americans particularly liked the anecdotes about Sir Winston Churchill and his dog, Rufus, and some of the celebrities whose pets I had treated. The switchboard was twice jammed with incoming calls, and I had a huge postbag for the rest of my stay in the States.

That was some day. After the show I had a lunchtime interview with Cleveland Amery, journalist, author, TV personality and the man who helped to found the American equivalent of our RSPCA. He was a charming man, and I was sorry when the interview ended.

Just before this very pleasant interlude, I learned what Americans call tomato juice for consumption on licensed premises. I was having pre-lunch drinks with Cleveland and some of his friends, and everyone was drinking vodka and tomato juice. The order went round the group, 'Bloody Mary, Bloody Mary, Bloody Mary, Virgin Mary . . .'

The Virgin Mary was for me – tomato juice without vodka! I was greatly amused. The Americans have mastered the art of the sophisticated, irreverent wisecrack and built it into their national character.

Just one hour later I was on my way to a reception and book-signing session at Arthur's, the discothèque just opened by Sybil Jordan, the former wife of Richard Burton, and her new young husband. I think the marriage was still in the honeymoon stage, because they didn't turn up as expected, but I did manage to meet the lovely Lauren Bacall again. Lauren, who was married to the late Humphrey

Bogart, was a great friend of Dorothy Pearson and of Rose, Marchioness of Headfort, who was once Rosie Boote, the Gaiety Girl. Poor Rosie, who is dead now, was a client of mine – or, rather, her beloved dachshunds were – and that was how I first met Lauren. So we had a lot to talk about.

We didn't get much time for a chat, though. The place was packed, the noise deafening, and the décor devilish. The dance floor was full of people, many of whom appeared to be making love on their feet. I signed hundreds of books and was glad to escape.

The next stop was a curious contrast – the Episcopal Church Centre radio station, of all places. I was received by what appeared to be a nun, then interviewed by the Reverend Dana Kennedy, a remote connection of the Kennedy clan. This was the toughest interview I had in America. The Reverend Kennedy started by asking me if I thought animals had souls. I told him yes. I said they had as much right to be on the earth as we had, that they did a great deal less damage, and many of them had an infinite capacity for love. I said they were as worthy of having a soul as we were, and in many cases a damn sight more worthy. He did not openly agree with me, but I could see he was impressed by the depth of my feelings. At one stage I had a horrible feeling that this man of God was trying to take the mickey, but I later learned that he was fond of animals himself and owned a dog and a couple of cats.

I still hadn't got through that incredible day. That evening Benny took me to a Broadway theatre to see *Mame*. I was dying to visit the loo, and was just about to issue the necessary instructions when the interval came and I was surrounded by hordes of people, most of whom had seen me on the 'Today' show.

It was the same at the end of the show. I had been invited backstage to meet Angela Lansbury, the British-born star of the show, and the rest of the cast, but by the time Benny and I had fought clear of the autograph hunters everyone had gone home to bed. I would dearly have loved to do likewise, but there was still one more engagement to round off that amazing day. I had to go for drinks at El Morocco, that fabulous night club. This had been one of my youthful ambitions, but by the time I got there I was almost too tired to care. But I perked up when I was introduced to Joan Crawford, a pin-up of mine since I was a teenager. It was still a thrill to meet her in person, and she looked absolutely lovely – surely the most beautiful woman of her generation. The El Morocco is a great place for celebrity goggling and I don't know who was getting the most attention, Joan or the Duke and Duchess of Windsor, who were showing their great skill on the dance floor.

Then it was bed at last. I slept like a log after the most hectic and exciting day of my life.

One hears that Americans can be brusque and even rude, but I only met one unpleasant character during the whole of the trip. The man was a famous television personality who shall, in deference to the laws of libel, remain nameless. He disliked me on sight. It was mutual! I think he was deliberately trying to ruffle me, because just before we went on he asked me if I really liked animals! I said, 'Yes, of course, haven't you read my book?'

'Yes, but I hate animals,' he replied.

I said, politely, 'Do you?'

'Yes,' he said, warming to his theme, 'if I saw a dog in my back yard I'd boot it. If I saw a cat, I'd shoot it.'

Charming, I thought, and then I noticed that what was obviously a toupee was slipping slightly from his head, giving him a drunken, rakish appearance. I didn't say a word, of course. I was praying that no one would notice it, and they didn't, so he went in front of the cameras looking like a victim of an Indian who had been interrupted in half-scalp, as it were. It was with great delight that I broke into a question to inform him sweetly that his slip was showing. The papers splashed the incident with great delight the following morning, and I must say I relished his embarrassment.

I had one free day in the three-week tour, and for that Benny gave up a day off and took me to a dog show in White Plains, Connecticut. But it wasn't a free day after all. I was asked to present the prizes, had to sign hundreds more autographs, and was badgered with questions about canine health. But it was all spontaneous and I really enjoyed it.

It came to an end at last. There was a final cocktail party at my hotel attended by all the people who had helped me and some friends I just hadn't had time to see. Benny bashfully gave me quite an expensive present and treated me to an extra special drive to the docks. My last impressions of New York passed in a blur of speed and dreadful language from Benny's arch enemies, the taxi drivers.

It seemed that America was as reluctant to release me as I was to leave. Crossing Fifth Avenue we were held up by the St Patrick's Day Parade which was in full swing. I have never seen so many battered silk top hats, or so much shamrock worn by one person, as on that day. The noise from the bands and the discord were ear-shattering but everyone was clearly enjoying themselves. Finally I got to the stateroom in the *Queen Mary* only to find another surprise party in progress. Amongst the guests were my old friend Honor Johnson and her doctor husband who had flown from Detroit to spend the last weekend in my hotel, and many American friends whom I had only been able to speak to on the telephone. But though the accents were American and the drink was champagne, I felt that the trip was over and that I was back on British soil. The *Queen Mary*, of course, was very British – one is tempted to say, too British. It was the ship's last voyage but one and the staff were all very depressed, a fact that was reflected in the service. And I thought the food was poor.

The great trip ended in a measure of irony. My first job on landing at Southampton was to go to the Southern ITV studios where I was interviewed about the American tour. The interviewer, Pat Solmas, was waiting for me with her team, and it was fascinating to compare the techniques of American and British television. Everything was much more relaxed and the pace had dropped to a more comfortable level.

Pat said how American I looked. I was clad in one of my new Saks suits, complete with hat, and I told her the American look could only be achieved at great expense. As I said this, I had a vivid impression of Benny gazing at me reproachfully, his big brown eyes as sad as a spaniel's . . .

I find it very true when one says New York overworks the adrenalin glands. It was all go but I thank God that I was able to cope with everything that came my way during the three weeks. It took me two weeks to unwind and get back to a normal routine in The Penthouse.

Chapter Three

TENERIFE AND MADEIRA

I first went to Tenerife many years ago on board a Bergen Line ship called the *Venus*. The ship waddled like an old goose and would have made heavy work of the Thames Estuary on a calm day. For this reason, she was known among the enlightened as the 'Vomiting Venus', and you can well imagine her antics in a gale in the Bay of Biscay. But her destination and ports of call made it all worth while. She called at Madeira, Las Palmas and Tenerife. The ship's photographer made the most of the exotic backgrounds – he was a talented young man then known as Tony Armstrong-Jones. We became quite friendly, and I learned that his London studio was near my surgery in Pimlico. I liked him from the start – we both had polio in common – and one of the things I most admire about him is the way he has refused to allow his currently exalted position to change his attitudes to life. I think that every time I meet him I get a fresh insight into his refusal to change. But I can't help thinking that sometimes he would find things a little easier if he conformed. . .

I remember once I had been persuaded to join a party going to a big fashion show for charity at Glyndebourne. I love the place and I love opera, but the rigours of hours at a stretch in my wheelchair had forced me to give up my membership. So it was a nostalgic occasion, tinged with sadness. The fashion show bored me to tears, and I was wriggling about as though my chair was red hot. When the time came for the champagne buffet in the glorious Music Room, I scooted along there with enthusiasm, urgently in need of a reviver.

Because I knew the layout of the place, I didn't line up in the crocodile of guests. It didn't dawn on me that there was to be an official reception until I arrived at one door and found Tony and Princess Margaret receiving people at the other. So I sat there like a lemon until eventually

Tony saw me and came over, leaving Princess Margaret to deal with the diminishing dribble of guests. We were having a chat when Her Royal Highness came over and stood staring at her husband's back. She did not exactly look the soul of patience. I broke into Tony's conversation and told him Her Royal Highness was waiting. She gave me a tiny glare – tiny, but concentrated. Tony, however, just carried on talking until he had finished.

I could not help sympathising a little with Princess Margaret. Squiring a beautiful woman imposes certain obligations – and when that woman is also royalty – well! I think she may have been entitled to feel niggly and neglected.

But to return to Tenerife. When I opened my love-hate relationship with the magical island, it was well before the days of the tourist explosion. Prices were ridiculously low, but so, I suppose, were the amenities. My very first night in Tenerife coincided with a power failure, which plunged the whole of Puerto de la Cruz into blackness. So it stayed until dawn came. The hotel did what it could with candles, but what with their dim light and the strangeness of the place, it was a weird start to Christmas.

It was a sad start, too. My first Christmas ever away from home and no friends around me – the only carols I heard were being played very badly in the hotel's dining-room on a badly tuned piano. Alas, I am a great sentimentalist, and 'Silent Night', rough but recognisable, nearly brought me to tears.

After dinner I went to church, a beautiful old church and very Catholic, naturally. Christmas Eve on the island is a bigger time than Christmas Day and it was a fascinating experience. The music came from banjos, accordions, every instrument you could think of, and people were coming in and prostrating themselves on the stone floor in homage. Some wore evening dress, like the plantation owners and visitors, while others were in rags.

The service went on for three hours, which is a bit much, and I was glad to be shown upstairs where the choir was ensconced in a little bird's-nest place. Close by a group of men, presumably not very devout churchgoers, were playing cards!

After the service, at around two o'clock in the morning, there was a torchlight procession all around the town, with the youngsters trooping into hotels and houses a bit like a supercharged version of the Helston floral dance. A strange way to start Christmas, I thought.

In those days, there were several things I didn't like about Tenerife, and I am afraid some of them haven't changed much to this day. I hated the food, for a start. I know it's a bit of a bore, but I am a vegetarian and I don't eat meat or fish. Unfortunately, sea food was the staple diet of the island, and positively everything was cooked in either fish oil or banana oil, bananas being the other staple. Even the poor old cows were not allowed to graze naturally, and were fed in stables on banana leaves and the unripe fruit, so even the milk tasted of bananas. In fact, everything tasted of bananas or fish.

I used to eat there very frugally, and share my hotel meals between the children, who appeared to be half starving, and the poor, unwanted animals, who certainly were starving. I lived on bread and bananas for three weeks and lost so much weight that I can recommend this fare as a good crash diet. I haven't eaten another banana to this day, incidentally. At least this kept me free for a time, however, from the dreaded 'Tenerife Tummy', a type of gastric fever that the Americans in Mexico call 'Montezuma's Revenge'. In the hotel foyer was a glass case containing numerous bottles of medicine, and, for extreme cases, ampoules of serum. The latter had to be administered by a doctor, and the disease was very debilitating.

I thought the food position really grim. One night I was taken to a small, typical Tenerife café. On the rocks outside, small boys were collecting limpets and little octopi and bringing them up to the bar where they were dipped in hot oil and eaten immediately. I am certain half of the creatures were not even dead, and that, plus a rough red wine that also tasted strongly of bananas, was not my idea of a gastronomic feast.

Because the food problem was so grim, I began looking forward to getting back on the old 'Vomiting Venus', where the food was excellent, if one could keep it down. But the minute I did get thankfully aboard, I went down immediately with 'Tenerife Tummy'. Thereafter, for five interminable days I lay in bed fighting both the bug and the usual sickness generated by the old *Venus*.

Actually, England would do me very nicely all the year round, if it were not for the fact that polio has affected my lungs, making me susceptible to pneumonia. I get it every winter as a matter of course, in the same way that practically everyone else gets a cold. When I get over it, I just have to recuperate in the sun.

I think I prefer Madeira to Tenerife, but in those days the landing daunted me. There is, of course, a fine modern harbour now, but I well remember the gymnastics one needed to land. The last time I went there, the ship anchored well out to sea because there wasn't sufficient depth close in and I was lowered over the side in a wicker basket, rather like an old goat. I remember Dorothy looking terrified as the basket full of me was swung down the side to a tiny launch, but I'm delighted to say that all went well. They didn't drop me.

They seem very fond of basketwork on Madeira. On that same trip I was carried from my hotel down a cliff to a swimming pool in a basketware rickshaw sort of thing, with one man fore and another aft. It was a laborious trip for them, and they had to carry me back again very soon because the heat from the sun was shattering. I retired to the safety of my balcony and stayed there most of *that* holiday.

One particularly good friend who now winters in Tenerife is Honor Johnson, a spectacular American blonde with a heart that matched the colour of her hair. Honor once played a starring role in probably one of the most amusing incidents of my life. I still laugh until I cry when I think about it. It happened one day when she was paying me a visit and I had arranged to meet her at Brighton Station.

One can drive right on to the platform at Brighton – I was able to drive in those days – and as I was parking my car, which was a white convertible, I saw a group of students carrying placards with '42 inches' plastered all over them. Now those were the dear, departed days when students wore glasses and sports jackets and worried frowns, and were far too busy studying to go to the cinema even, so I thought it a little strange. I inquired, and was told that they, with some municipal celebrities, were waiting to meet Sabrina, a young lady widely celebrated for her frontage, which was imposing, to say the least. The reference to '42 inches' was the measurement of her achievements. And Sabrina, apparently, was coming to Brighton to launch a big shopping week.

The London train arrived, and Honor was one of the first off. She strode towards me, her coiffure a masterpiece of the peroxide fantasia; a statuesque and purposeful figure.

As I hurried her to my car, before the mob saw Sabrina, I heard the students chanting, 'Let's have a look,' and 'I'll measure 'em,' and other vulgarities one did not then associate with degree courses in the Arts.

As we drove away, I had a sudden, ghastly premonition. And sure enough, two police motor-cyclists flanked my car and other vehicles, including the mayoral Daimler, formed up in line astern. One of the cars contained the late Gilbert Harding, that well known and distinguished performer, who was improbably clad in a Norfolk jacket. They thought Honor was Sabrina!

We were well into Brighton by the time the mess sorted itself out and the cortège disengaged and raced back to the station. I often wonder if Sabrina was left standing forlornly on the platform, or whether they got back in time. I also wonder what Gilbert Harding thought about the whole business. He had a superb range of glares, deep breathing, bottled fury and mottled blood pressure. I am glad I was out of range when he brought the big guns to bear.

It was in Tenerife on a later occasion that poor Dena Dene arrived. And when that loving little terrier bitch made the first overtures of friendship, I was not to know that she was to make this holiday happy and a subsequent one very sad . . .

An American friend, whose only drawback was that she disliked animals, joined us at the Casa we had rented from a Dutch surgeon. And when a little terrier arrived in the garden one day, our friend chased it off. At the time, I must say I thought this was probably the best thing to do – it isn't fair to make a fuss and feed other people's dogs.

But she came again, day after day, once panting and obviously distressed. I realised she was a stray and that she was very thirsty. So we gave her a drink – and that was it. She was ours for the next ten weeks. She moved in with enthusiasm, and we called her Dena Dene. I have always called my dogs something to do with Denes (my kennel prefix) and Dena seemed to suit her. But very soon after her arrival, I realised she was sickening for something. That something turned out to be hard pad. She very nearly died. She was so weak and ill she could hardly move. Her eyes were thick, her nose was crusted over and she became as thin as a rake. She had a raging fever and her temperature reached 105 degrees. I had some herbal remedies with me, so I gave her garlic tablets to cleanse her digestive system and greenleaf tablets to help purify her blood stream. During the next week, she was given only honey and boiled water and no solid foods. Twice a day we cleansed her eyes and mouth with liquid garlic and kept her nasal passages clear. Dorothy, Ron and I took turns in nursing her day and night, and gradually she fought her way out of danger.

The next task was to build her up – the hard pad had left her incredibly thin. I put her on a special diet of meat and fish, and she ate everything we put before her.

I am as familiar as most people with that thrill of pleasure one gets from nursing a dying animal back to health, but there was something about Dena – something special. She was the highlight of my holiday. Soon, she had perked up enough to get a little naughty – a sure sign of recovery in a dog. She would lie by the fire at night and nibble the bobbles off the armchairs when we weren't looking. Dorothy would sew them on again in the mornings.

Dorothy, like me, is a true animal lover, but our American friend behaved very badly about Dena. If a person dislikes dogs, or any other animal, because of a natural aversion or fear, I can understand and sympathise. But the American disliked Dena partly because the dog was a mongrel, and partly because of a deep-rooted and almost pathological jealousy. She told me once that she hated a dog owned by her husband so violently that she gave him an ultimatum: either the dog goes or I do. He was devoted to the dog, but went out and shot it. I personally feel he would have been much happier with the dog! He died suddenly shortly afterwards.

The last time I saw this woman was when she visited us in England. She said she quite liked Digger Dene, my golden retriever, and Puggy the pug, because they were pedigree. Thus she compounded snobbery with jealousy.

As the holiday progressed, I began to worry about what would happen to Dena when we returned to England. I took her to all the social functions in the hope that somebody would adopt her. I took her to church – a very social occasion – and all the ladies in their big hats and white gloves would admire her. But nobody wanted her.

In all fairness, I must point out that most of the English colony only wintered in Tenerife. Many of them had homes elsewhere with dogs of their own. They were not being callous, just practical. As for me, I had fallen for Dena completely, and began to think hard about taking her home with me. A friend of mine, Eric Sawyer, now managing director of Denes, has his own quarantine kennel and said he would take her at a reduced fee. I hate putting dogs in quarantine, but there was no alternative and I resolved to do this. The time would soon pass, and I could picture Dena romping with Puggy on the lawn at home. Anyway, I knew Eric's kennels were beautifully run and that Dena would be treated as well as if she was at home with us. But it was not to be. There was an epidemic of rabies at Camberley, panic spread and an order was issued – no dogs to be allowed into England.

Poor Dena Dene. She was so loyal and good, I couldn't imagine anybody *not* wanting her. I intensified my efforts to find her a good home. One very suitable family almost took her, but changed their minds when they learned there was no trace of alsatian in her – a curious reversal. Many people suspect a mongrel with an alsatian in the background. Finally, when time had almost run out, I was told of an American lady who was looking for a dog. She saw Dena, and to my delight agreed to have her. I checked her home and was a little worried to find the garden unfenced, but right next door was a bull terrier called Bill. Bill and Dena became great friends, during Bill's visits to us to be de-ticked. When we finally sailed for home, my sadness at parting with Dena was diminished at the thought that she had a good home.

My first job on getting back to Brighton was to write to Dena's new owner and send her natural health remedies and diet supplements and feeding charts and hints and tips on keeping dogs. The letter was never answered. Time went by and our other letters were ignored. Eventually, I heard from the Lemon Man – a neighbour who used to give us fresh lemons – that he had seen Dena running through the streets in Puerto. She seemed healthy, and had apparently been

adopted by a German woman. I learned later that the American woman had not locked Dena up securely, and she had escaped the very day we sailed. I had told her most clearly to keep Dena indoors for a few days until she got used to her new home.

I'm sorry, but this story has a sad ending. I learned later that Dena was seen very much in whelp, then, two months later, she was rounded up in one of the island's periodic stray-dog drives and certainly put to sleep.

I will never forget Dena Dene. I wish so much I had been able to bring her back to England.

To get back to a more cheerful topic like pneumonia. I had it again in 1971, and once more, on the doctor's orders, I set forth with Ron again for Tenerife in January. This time we stayed at an hotel. It was one of those which has sprung up like a mushroom, almost overnight, and it was inordinately high. I found myself on the 15th floor. Now this was not so good. I *hate* lifts. I have to sit there in my wheelchair, everyone else stands around looking wooden, it stops at every single floor, and all those healthy lungs commandeer all the oxygen before I get my share. I also have a horror of being stuck in a lift with a jammed door, or one which has broken down between floors. And one final point: if you are in a wheelchair in a lift in Tenerife, you will find that your head is just about tummy high to the other standing occupants. Most of these occupants have stomachs bulging over bikinis and trunks – dress is very informal on the island.

So I sit there like Buddha, contemplating other people's navels. I promise you this is a singularly unrewarding experience. I could write a technical manual on the navels of Tenerife and make a reasonably accurate guess as to the nationality of the owner. (For instance, French girls have chic navels, as though the doctor who attended their birth gave them a sexy start in life. German men have coarse navels, peering out like Cyclops from the expanse of their bellies. British girls have discreet, non-committal navels, as undistinguished as a semi-detached in Purley.)

With the exception of the lift problem, this was an unremarkable holiday. But I did see a male puppy which reminded me strongly of Dena. Could it be . . .?

I honestly don't know. The age was about right, and he had Dena's eyes and looks, and that is all I can say.

Chapter Four

A VET IN PARIS

For many years, Paris was to play a wonderful part in my life. I ran there what my friends called the 'Robin Hood' clinic – they said that I robbed the rich to pay for the poor. I do not think this description completely justified – I hate the 'robbed' bit – but it is a fact that my part-time veterinary practice in Paris had amongst its clients the very rich and the very poor, and that my fees from the rich paid for the free side of the practice, which, believe me, was considerable.

But I'm getting ahead of myself. Let's begin at the beginning.

It was just after the war when I received a letter postmarked Paris. I opened it, and it was from a Mme Goldschmidt-Halot. Would I please come over immediately and treat her poodle, Laurette? When I thought about it, that unusual name rang a bell. I remembered receiving a letter from someone of the same name just before the war. I went back through my files and found the letter. It was from the same person. They had asked me to come over and attend the whelping – the letter called it 'accouchement' – of their poodle! I would have done, but the war intervened in its very tiresome way. I surmised (correctly, as it turned out) that Laurette was one of that pre-war litter. I wrote back saying that I was going on holiday to St Tropez shortly, and would pop in and see them in Paris on my way back. Which is exactly what I did.

M. and Mme Goldschmidt-Halot lived in a glorious apartment in the Boulevard Lannes overlooking the Bois de Boulogne. The husband was Jewish, and the couple had had a very hard time during the war.

They had lived quietly for some time after the German occupation, but as things got tougher they were forced to flee, and thereafter were constantly on the move, keeping just one jump ahead of the Gestapo. They left three poodles behind in the care of their chauffeur, but the Germans found out and commandeered the apartment, kicking the dogs out into the Bois and shooting them down. The Germans also found the apartment an irresistible plum, with its gorgeous paintings and rich wine-cellar. When the Goldschmidt-Halots returned with Laurette, who had shared all their hardships, they found chaos. The whole place had been pillaged. The wines, of course, had gone, and so had the paintings. They had expected this, but what really shook them was the degree of useless vandalism – and from German officers who had been billeted there. The carved oak panelling in the main rooms had been ripped off the walls and burned in open fires in the middle of the rooms. The padded tapestries had been slashed by bayonets and utterly ruined.

Looting is part of the fortunes of war. 'C'est la guerre,' as the French say, shrugging with Gallic resignation. But the degree of utterly senseless vandalism appalled the couple, who nevertheless counted themselves extremely fortunate to survive the war with much of their fortune left, secure in the vaults of a Swiss bank.

When I first saw them, their apartment, which had many rooms, was more like a block of flats. Accommodation in Paris was at a premium and, as a condition of reoccupying their home, the Goldschmidt-Halots had to fill their rooms with 'temporaries' – there was the ex-chauffeur, his wife and two daughters; and their cook, her mother and sister. Their daughter's old nanny was in residence, plus the governess and her husband.

It was particularly difficult for the Goldschmidt-Halots to abide the presence of the chauffeur. They couldn't prove it, of course, but there were definite indications that it was he who informed the Germans that M. Goldschmidt-Halot was a Jew. The man was very much the ex-chauffeur, but in the absence of conclusive proof, there was nothing else they could do – they had to tolerate his presence under the same roof!

When I arrived there, it was a saint's day – I can't remember which one because they have so many in France – and I can vividly remember the cook trying to make crêpes suzettes with egg powder. The coffee was ersatz and made mainly from acorns. It was quite vile, and I longed for a cup of English tea. It was also the family's first 'at home' since the occupation, so the place was full of people looking very shabby wearing what was once the height of fashion. It was rather sad, in a way, but encouraging too, to see a cross-section of a whole stratum of society picking up the threads and starting their lives all over again.

After the meal, bravely attempted, but rather awful, I examined Laurette and found that she was suffering from a serious deficiency of vitamins. But she was a lovely bitch, and no amount of malnutrition could hide her superb breeding. I had brought no medicines with me, but I didn't really need any. Given an hour in the countryside, I could select from nature's bountiful medicine cupboard the cures for many ailments.

And this is what I did. The following day, I took the couple into the country around Neuilly and showed them what herbs to give the dog. They were so enthusiastic at this illustration of the naturopath's art that they asked me to write out a little descriptive catalogue, identifying the herbs and listing their benefits. I found out afterwards that they 'treated', if that is the word, dozens of children too. Practically everyone was suffering from deficiencies in those days. The bitch started to recover almost immediately, and the Goldschmidt-Halots were overcome with gratitude. They would ring me weekly after I returned, reporting progress and telling me which of their friends' children were recovering, helped by an intake of natural vitamins.

As France began to totter back to prosperity after the German rape, pre-war dog societies were re-formed and the first of the post-war shows began. They showed Laurette, and she began to win prizes.

One day, they rang me, and asked me to come over to Paris and select a suitable sire for the bitch. I thought she was a little long in the tooth for breeding, but decided it would be all right. I toured some of the kennels which were gradually re-emerging, and finally found a dog I considered would be a suitable sire. Nine weeks after the mating, I returned to attend the whelping, but when I landed in France, I realised my assistant had forgotten to pack my instruments. I thought that I must have them, because I was still a trifle worried about Laurette's age. Frantic phone calls ensued, and my instruments were finally flown out by BEA.

They were necessary, as it turned out. I had to induce the birth and help Laurette to deliver. But it all turned out very happily. Laurette had four beautiful puppies and went on to become supreme champion of France and international champion as well. The original strain is still going strong and has produced many champions.

Through the Goldschmidt-Halots, I met a considerable proportion of Paris society, most of whom were dog or cat lovers. It was from one such person that I was recommended to a professor who specialised in the chest. I saw him and was persuaded to undergo a course of treatment. As this meant I was to be periodically in Paris, the Goldschmidt-Halots offered me the use of a small suite in their apartment. Soon word spread that I was willing to treat animals – so I ran an occasional clinic, fees from the wealthy subsidising my work for the animals of the poor; hence the Robin Hood description. I personally never made a sou's profit from this. But I loved the work: it made a pleasant change from my practice in England and helped to pay for my treatment in France.

When I think back, it must have been the most curious practice in veterinary history, and my clinic was surely the most exclusive vet's premises ever. (Above me, in fact, was a vastly successful gynaecologist. I used to treat his Skye terriers, which were the most superb specimens of the breed I have ever seen.) But not all my patients had pedigrees by any means. The concierge downstairs had a mongrel, which I used to treat, together with those of many friends. I made some good friends among White Russian taxi drivers and treated their pets too. The word got around, and I was frequently inundated with little *garçons* with pooches on strings.

It was a *most* democratic practice. The surgery was a superb room, with moulded ceiling and a chandelier. The furniture was Louis Quatorze and Quinze, and my assistant, gentle and very enthusiastic, was none other than Mme

Goldschmidt-Halot – a friend of Pope Pius XII and intimate of the Bourbons. It was all very, very different from back home!

I had some wonderful friends in Paris. One of my favourite characters was a slender, dark and very voluble man called Raymond Massiett, a leading light in the resistance movement in Paris and a man who lived on his enormous reserves of nervous energy. Raymond was an actuarial impossibility – a man who had taken as many risks as he should, by all the laws of probability, have been killed several times. But Raymond survived – and he survived a post-war crisis, too. Some of his exploits and escapes are legendary. There are five places in Paris with commemorative plaques to the effect that Massiett stayed there under various aliases.

I lunched with Raymond and his wife once and they took me to a subway underneath their apartment which still contained an ancient printing-press. This worked all through the war, printing all sorts of pamphlets and literature, and the Germans never discovered it. It must have been a terrible strain living above that all the time, particularly since he was the most wanted man in France.

On one occasion he was being chased by the Gestapo and dodged up a side street just off the Champs-Elysées. Raymond was almost cornered when he saw a woman sitting by herself at a café table. He sat down next to her and seized an empty glass. The woman responded magnificently and passed him her lighted cigarette before taking another for herself. As the Gestapo ran round the corner they saw no fugitive – just a pair of lovers enjoying a drink and a smoke in a typical Paris setting. They ran on past and the crisis was over. Raymond often said he would love to meet the woman again and thank her.

I first met him in Calvi, Corsica. He was lying on the beach with two other resistance veterans – both girls! – and Robert Carrier, who was virtually unknown at the time. We started talking, and the bitterest topic was the fact that there was no electricity and hence no ice anywhere in the town. But for all that we adjourned to a bar and made do with a warm drink.

We all met several times. We were on the beach together

one day when a dazzlingly white, but rather old fashioned, yacht sailed into harbour with none other than General de Gaulle on board. Raymond was absolutely delighted. He was an old friend of de Gaulle – a friendship forged during the war when the General was the spirit of French resistance and Raymond and his gallant colleagues were its sword.

He sent a note to the yacht and a meeting was arranged in a place called the American Bar. I remember that I was not particularly impressed with the man. He was very tall, aloof and austere. He was undoubtedly a great man, but hardly the life and soul of the party. Raymond revered him, which made subsequent events even harder to understand . . .

I returned to England after that particular holiday, but was soon to meet Raymond again in the strangest circumstances. I was boarding a normal flight from London to Le Bourget when I saw Anna Neagle and her husband, Herbert Wilcox, in a distinguished-looking party, which included two gentlemen who looked familiar. They were Trevor Howard and Peter Ustinov. The tiny woman keeping quietly in the background was Odette, and her escort was her husband, Peter Churchill.

I gathered Anna and the party were going to attend the première of her new film, *Odette*, in which she played the title rôle. The film was to be shown that night at the Opéra in aid of a gigantic appeal fund for the relatives of resistance workers who gave their lives.

When the plane landed I emerged, feeling rather guilty at treading on a red carpet, and saw none other than Raymond, festooned in medals and orders, who was heading the official reception with a brass band playing 'La Marseillaise' in the background. Raymond greeted me as if I was one of the party, and planted two garlicky kisses on my face. He insisted that I join the celebrations. So I joined the entourage, and we were all whisked away in several limousines to Raymond's immense apartment for a champagne buffet. Raymond quickly organised a dinner suit for me, but I remember it had a frilly shirt – very French but not really me.

France was just emerging from a period of post-war austerity, and the women at the reception were magnificently gowned. All the dresses had Dior or Balenciaga stamped on them, and I thought then that only Paris could produce such magnificent women and dress them accordingly.

After the party, we all proceeded to the Opéra, and never, as long as I live, will I forget the emotion of one moment. Odette walked slowly up the noble staircase, and on every step stood a hero of the resistance. Some of these, men and women, had an arm or a leg missing, many were scarred about the face; one man had a swastika branded on his forehead. The tiny figure of Odette, dressed in a simple full-length dress, was dwarfed by her wartime colleagues, who stood as erect as guardsmen on parade. In the light from the fantastic chandeliers I could see she was quietly crying, and so were many of the men. It was a terribly emotional experience.

Before the film started, Raymond and Odette walked hand in hand on to the stage. The applause was thunderous. All around me strong men were crying. With tears that night the men and women of the Maquis remembered their fallen compatriots.

I very much admired the behaviour of Anna Neagle at those moments. She stayed firmly in the background. Dear Anna knew she was only acting the part – Odette had played it for real. What a wonderful job Anna had made of it; she told me later that it was the favourite part she had played.

For quite a time, Raymond did very well after the war. He ran a school, and inherited a title, the Marquis du Keuguelin de Rozier, a château and all that goes with it from his father whom he met as he was dying – Raymond had been brought up on the outskirts of Paris by his mother and until then given to believe his father was a butcher. The course of his life was running smoothly and prosperously until he tried to assassinate General de Gaulle. He was caught presiding over a murderous ambush comprising five men, all armed with machine-guns. The entire party were pledged to shoot the General on his way to work. Inevitably a long term of imprisonment followed. Thus did the game of politics rupture a link forged when France was fighting for her very life.

Raymond was let out eventually, I'm delighted to say, and has now settled down as squire of his village, based in his fabulous thirteenth-century château complete with spires, turrets and a circular moat.

My car broke down once near Chartres, quite close to Raymond's château. I phoned him and a rescue party arrived. For four nights I slept in a chamber that hadn't changed much in 500 years. It had stone floors, slit windows designed to keep out arrows, and my bed was a four-poster.

Raymond took his duties very seriously. As the local equivalent of the squire, one of his duties was to precede the village to church every Sunday. He did it, although he thought it a bit of a bore. It was very different from his former day-to-day existence, when he lived on his guile and his reflexes and his nerves.

I had one terrifying experience in Paris. I had been made an honorary member of the French Gun Dog Society, and like all French investitures the ceremony was attended by champagne, lots of delightful food and an equal number of boring speeches. I finally tottered out of the hotel, feeling thoroughly invested, and walked right into a mob of people. A Communist riot was in progress, and I was carried away, like a piece of driftwood in a powerful current. We surged down Rue Royale to the Madeleine, where massed ranks of police, many on horses, stood by with batons drawn and water cannons at the ready. Then the police charged with more verve than their forefathers had at Agincourt. Batons rose and fell, horses reared and students scattered like quail.

By this time I was badly frightened. This was of course before the time I had to take to a wheelchair, but I had my leg irons on and I was not exactly nimble. I had great difficulty keeping on my feet and I knew that if once I fell down I could very well be trodden to death.

Working on the premise that it is folly to fight directly against the current, I began to work my way through the mob diagonally. Eventually, I managed to 'divert' myself through a smashed plate-glass window to safety.

When things had quietened down, I began to walk slowly back. Just outside the British Embassy, I saw another crowd. But it wasn't a demonstration – just a crowd waiting to see

Princess Margaret and her escort leaving the building after a reception. I waited too. She looked so radiant. The following day the papers were full of the fact that she had gone to a night club. The tone of the reports, without actually saying anything, conveyed a distinct impression that something a little naughty had occurred. Nothing had, of course, but French journalists are masters at the art of the veiled innuendo, while some of their readers could read something improper into *Pilgrim's Progress*.

It was during my time in Paris that I cemented my friendship with Bob Carrier. In fact I was staying with Bob at his apartment in the Avenue de la Bourdonnière when I was caught up with the riot.

During our first meeting in Paris, I thought Bob's American-style camelhair overcoat was marvellous. He, in turn, wanted a cocker spaniel. So a trade was arranged. I returned to England resplendent in the coat, and came back again a month later with a golden cocker which Bob called Poppett and loved for many years. It was just as well we arranged the swap, because my overcoat had been stolen days earlier in most mysterious circumstances.

I parked the car outside the Hotel Georges Cinq to meet some friends. I locked the car as usual, and left my overcoat – a brand new Crombie – inside. Like a fool, I left my passport in the overcoat pocket. When I returned, I unlocked the car, climbed in – and found my coat was missing. Somehow, the thief had unlocked the door, as opposed to breaking in, stolen the coat, along with the car lighter, the hooter button and the tax disc, and then locked up again securely.

But here is the mystery. He took my passport out of the pocket and slipped it down beside the seat. I will never know why. In those days, passports were worth their weight in gold and fetched large sums of money in criminal circles. Quite possibly, in fact, the passport was worth more than the car. I mourned for my new overcoat, but could not have cared less about the other trivia that were stolen. Was he a kind thief, I often wonder, sparing me the embarrassment of being passportless in France?

In those days, Bob's apartment was what we would call a mews flat. It was situated in an inner courtyard, behind a block of buildings, in what was once a big stable. He had done it out himself and the décor was sensational – so much so that friends brought their friends to see it and Bob became something of a social lion on the strength of his home. If he had not been an expert in the culinary arts, he would have made a most successful interior decorator or a *haute couture* designer.

His job at the time was to write, direct and produce a radio programme on the lives of Americans in Paris. The programme was broadcast in America three times a week and had a huge following. Bob interviewed American stars and celebrities travelling in France, and his knowledge of show business was encyclopaedic. But despite this, he threw up the job to run the American Theatre in Pigalle, and you could say he suffered for his art. He went from affluence to the breadline very quickly, and he and his helpers used to sleep at the theatre and live on bread and cheap wine.

The first production at the American Theatre must have been one of the most sensational first nights ever. A musical comedy was being staged, and the audience was packed with celebrities, including Erich von Stroheim, Gloria Swanson and Billie Holliday. The curtain was just about to rise when the gendarmes arrived. Could they inspect monsieur's fire insurance or the fire safety precautions, please? As it happened, they couldn't, because Bob had neither. An observance of rules and regulations was never one of Bob's strong points. The police refused to let the show go on. Monsieur Carrier was forbidden to lift the curtain. Then they departed, leaving one of their men behind to see that orders were obeyed. This could have been a death-blow to the American Theatre. Their total resources were currently contained in the box-office – enough money to pay off all the bills and finance the next production. What could be done?

Bob was equal to the occasion. He went on stage and told the audience of a technical hitch. He promised that in one hour's time an alternative show would be presented on the tiny strip of stage that was left in front of the curtain, and if they were not delighted with the entertainment, they could get their money back. The audience was not fully mollified. Then Erich von Stroheim saved the day by ascending the stage and telling everyone: 'To the bar. The drinks are on me.'

I was pressed into service as barman, and worked like a slave. Everyone who ordered a single anything got a double. Anyone who wanted a double got a treble. We dispensed liquid happiness as a matter of insurance. Bob, meanwhile, grabbed a taxi and made a lightning tour of the cafés and cabarets of Paris, everywhere where American artists were appearing. Such was the magic of his personality – and his reputation as a publicist – that he returned with three taxi-loads of performers.

While he was away, the thirsting hordes had just about drunk the bar dry, so Erich von Stroheim took a frightening chance and asked everyone to go back to their seats, telling them the show was about to go on. To fill in, he asked an almost unknown café singer to entertain. The tiny waif of a woman agreed. She sang six songs before Bob came back with the reinforcements. One of them – 'La Vie en Rose' – was the hit of the evening.

Her name was Edith Piaf.

The show was a sensational success. It was a fabulous evening and went on until three in the morning. No one demanded their money back, and practically everyone came back soon afterwards to see the original show. It didn't take Bob long to sort out the fire insurance problems with a handful of francs.

That evening was the first time I met Edith Piaf. Years later, when she became a superstar, she bought a huge house in the Boulevard Lannes, just four doors away from the Goldschmidt-Halots.

Poor Piaf. She had a very hard life and didn't live long enough really to enjoy the fruits of her success. I admired her tremendously, but I don't think she approved of me very much.

'Buster,' she told me once, 'you treat dogs better than a lot of people get treated . . .'

She was often very bitter. But the Little Sparrow, as she was known, had suffered a lot of rough handling herself. Perhaps she had good reason to be wary.

Chapter Five

ABOUT CATS

Whenever I write about cats I find it very difficult to generalise. I know of no area where cats merge into just cats – they are all clearly defined as characters. I don't wonder the Egyptians used to worship the fey, fickle, feline gods. Cats are so self-contained I often think they consider they keep us. Yet they can be wonderful companions when they feel like it. And they are so unpredictable – dogs by comparison are as easily read as a first form primer. I knew a cat which used to ambush the postman every morning, changing tactics and location like a guerrilla fighter, and another which used to catch mackerel and swim for pleasure. I even had a cat which thought he was a dog.

It is significant and perfectly in order that my first cat of childhood was a rarity. He was called Rufus – a big, handsome tabby with an aggressive clump of whiskers. Rufus had been brought up with dogs since he was a tiny kitten, and he had a certain psychological defect: Rufus thought he was a dog – albeit a very superior and agile dog.

When we played ball in the garden with the dogs, Rufus joined in. He was the only feline retriever in the business and widely celebrated in the area. He couldn't manage an old tennis ball, so he had a special one of his own. Heaven help the dog that beat him to it. Rufus would dash up and go 'pop, pop, pop' on the dog's nose with his left paw and dribble the ball neatly away with his right.

But despite the fact he thought he was a dog, Rufus would not hesitate to use his innate feline superiority as often as possible. He would ghost in like a shadow, steal a chunk of meat from under a dog's nose, then fly up a tree and eat it in peace and security. Only once did I see him nonplussed. One day he climbed a telegraph pole and became stuck. The fire brigade brought him down but he knew he had lost face.

Yet for all his schizophrenia, Rufus was indubitably a

cat. And that's the great virtue of cats. Whatever they think they are, they always retain that spark of independence and absolute incorruptibility which makes them so different from dogs. Actually, cats and dogs are not such deep-rooted enemies as many people think. A cat is superior to a dog in all departments except bulk, and I think both parties are aware of this. Most chases are enjoyed by all concerned, and few dogs will press matters if they have the luck (?) to corner a cat. There are exceptions to this. Some breeds, and very occasionally an individual dog from a normally 'pro-cat' breed, are cat killers, and I have treated cats with terrible injuries inflicted by dogs. The biggest sinners in this department are terriers, and particularly those who have the terrier's tenacity coupled with a powerful bulk.

There must be many thousands of cases of cat-dog friend-ship on record, but the most curious I ever experienced was a cat which fostered litters of pups. A very good friend of mine runs a large farm at Plumpton, near the gorgeous Sussex racecourse. He is a noted breeder of boxers and French bulldogs and has produced many champions. On the farm was a cat. It was practically wild and certainly not a house cat, sleeping in a barn and living off the land. She really was a wild and wary little creature who treated the farm like a jungle. Yet, whenever one of the boxers pro-duced a litter, the cat got as maternal as a natural mother. She would move in, and help the mother clean the puppies, topping and tailing them in their bed with her little rasp of a tongue.

On one occasion, my farmer friend rang me up and asked me to come out to the farm. 'I want you to confirm something. It's the strangest thing I've ever seen,' he said. Having fin-ished my appointments, I drove over, consumed with curio-sity. Arriving there I discovered that the cat had even lactated and was physically feeding two French bulldog puppies, while their poor old mum, who had run dry, looked on approvingly. I examined the cat and found her to be functioning in exactly the same manner as a nursing mum. Yet she wasn't anything of the kind. I know all about phantom pregnancies, but this was carried on to a most illogical conclusion. She fed the pups perfectly satisfactorily until they were weaned, after which she lost interest and went back to her near-predatory state, killing mice and birds. That cat was unique in my experience.

Another exceptional cat lived on the Scilly Isles, that charming group of islands which has been identified with Avalon of King Arthur fame, and more recently with Mr Harold Wilson. The cat's owners had rebelled against the rat race and had done something about it. They sold up in London and bought a cottage on St Mary's. He acquired a boat and went fishing, while his wife ran a smallholding and raised a few pigs and chickens. They kept a cow for milk, and took in guests during the summer and thus lived a happy and self-contained life.

On moving, they took with them their pampered, ultra-domesticated Persian cat called Ozymandias – or Oz for short. And Oz took to country life like a duck to water. He also took to water like a duck. I understand that one day Oz just walked down to the beach which was near by, paddled out into the water and started to swim, just like that! His next eccentricity was to accompany his master in the boat on all fishing trips. When the mackerel were shoaling and the boat was knee-deep in the shining, silvery fish, Oz used to lurk round the fringes picking out stragglers.

His most celebrated episode occurred on a calm day when the sea was as flat as a pancake. The boat was heavily laden with mackerel, and as it neared the beach the shallows were alive with an enormous shoal. Oz was perched in the bow in his usual position like a figurehead. As the boat was a few yards off the sand, he leaped into the sea and landed with a mackerel flapping in his mouth.

News of Oz filtered back to the mainland. A reporter and photographer from one of the county newspapers went there and did a picture story on Oz, swimming strongly for home with a mackerel in his mouth. This picture, which appeared in many national newspapers, was rigged. Neither the mackerel nor Oz were co-operative, so the cat was given a dead fish and carefully put over the side of a boat, while the photographer stood by in a skiff. It was based on fact, so I suppose it was permissible. Trust the cat to be awkward, though!

It's because cats are so self-contained and so little trouble to keep that so many people in the theatre are fans of *felis domestica,* as the Romans used to put it.

Actors have to be adaptable, and so do their pets. Dame Anna Neagle has a cat, an ordinary, low-born moggy which was born on the other side of the tracks, way off the tourist beat, in darkest Brighton. This cat adopted Anna, as cats do, and it took the transition from alley to luxury apartment, from fish heads to pâté, completely in its stride. It was a beautiful cat with a small, sensitive head, pink nose and a fluffy, black, tan and white coat that always looked as if it had been shampooed, blow-dried and back-combed. She would walk with a sensuous grace – for all the world like a superior and most expensive Parisienne model. I called her Frou-Frou, after the celebrated lady of pleasure in the Moulin Rouge.

One night, Anna kindly presented us with the royal box at the London theatre where she was starring in that long running musical, *Charley Girl.* After the show, Anna joined us for refreshments. With Anna, looking as if she had been born to the purple, was Frou-Frou, the alley cat fallen on good times. She was quite at home in the royal box ante-room. What a lucky cat she is!

Another actress who loves cats is Margot Bryant – Minnie Caldwell of *Coronation Street* fame. She lives near me at Hove, and Margot is an inveterate 'cat-talker'. When she sees a cat she talks to it in a private language, but whatever it is the cat seems to understand, and it is an undisputed fact that cats like Margot, too.

Margot is quite a character. She cultivates lots of indoor plants, and she talks to these as well. I find it hilarious when Margot crouches down and tells a plant in a broad, northern accent: 'Eh, cum on, rubber tree, stop sulking and grow.' They usually do as they are told.

It is a well-known fact that dogs are an occupational hazard of the postman's life. All postmen get bitten at some stage, but if the same postman is bitten by the same dog every day, then the Post Office will either resort to the law or cease delivering letters to that particular house.

I knew of a cat once that caused consternation in the

Post Office right up to regional headquarters level. The cat in question was a nondescript black and white tabby, dearly beloved by her owner, an elderly, somewhat eccentric woman who lived in a large country house near Tunbridge Wells. She was very wealthy, had no surviving relatives, and did the traditional thing and left a fortune to several cats' homes when she died. One of this lady's hobbies was to telephone me at least once a week, insisting that I come out and treat the cat for a variety of complaints, all of which were entirely imaginary. She rang me one day in a state of great alarm. 'Mr Lloyd-Jones,' she demanded, 'is it possible to de-claw a cat?' I told her it was unthinkable. 'Oh dear,' she said, 'then I shall be prosecuted.'

It turned out that one morning the postman had walked up the overgrown drive to her front door to be greeted by eight pounds of feline fury descending upon him from a tree. The cat scratched his neck, and departed. He took no action that day, and completed his rounds, doubtless considering that a postman's lot is not a happy one. The following day he walked up the drive again and the cat leaped out from ambush and had a brief go at his blue-serge trouser leg. Then, like a member of the Viet Cong, it melted back into the undergrowth. This time, he rang the bell and complained. The old lady was rude to him – she was to most people, incidentally – and he departed in a huff. But he still didn't file a complaint; I expect the Post Office has no forms governing attacks on postmen by cats.

There was no mail for two days, but the following morning there was another foul, feline attack. This time the cat got him on his way back down the drive – a nice, psychological touch, that! – and scratched his hand quite deeply. That was it. He complained long and loud, and accepted the jeers of his colleagues with fortitude. Rural postmen have been chased by cows, attacked by geese and stung by bees, but never in the annals of Post Office history has a postman been systematically terrorised by a moggy.

I can picture the furore the complaint must have caused. Phone calls were made, regulations turned up, and doubtless the police were contacted to see if there was such an offence as failing to keep a cat under proper control. The result was a personal visit by an official to the old lady with the polite suggestion that if she couldn't control her cat, she could collect her mail personally from the Post Office.

Why did her cat behave like that? Even if the postman had kicked it or slung a stone at it once, reprisals like that would have been excessive. I have known dogs bite a particular person on sight, but never a cat.

The upshot of all this was that the old lady kept her beloved cat under lock and key every morning until the mail was safely delivered. As far as I know, there was never a repeat of the ambuscades.

Will cats bear a grudge? I think, yes. But the usual course with cats and dogs who have been ill-treated by someone is for them to fear and avoid that someone. Most dogs will turn only as a last resort.

If I have learned one thing about cats in my life, I have learned the folly of trying to keep a cat anywhere it does not want to be. That includes wicker-baskets, rooms, and no doubt the maximum security wing of a prison. All cats have a natural talent for escapology. It used to worry me dreadfully whenever I had a cat in for lengthy treatment. One could reassure owners as much as one liked, but I knew with a fearful certainty that keeping a cat was purely a matter of luck.

In the field of feline escapology, one cat in particular would have won high international honours. It was a British Blue called Carlo and I would have backed him against Houdini any day. Carlo would disappear, dematerialise himself at will. And he caused me considerable trouble. Carlo's owners – or, rather, the people with whom Carlo chose to reside – brought him around once as he was suffering from a nasty skin trouble. They had children, and couldn't cope, and I thought a few days' treatment in my cattery was called for. I worked out a special vitaminised diet and dressed his sore places. Carlo was as good as gold, and took it all without a murmur. I put it down to a basic sweetness of nature, but I know now that Carlo wished only to lull me into a sense of false security. I put him in the cattery. His room was large with tree trunks set in the floor and old armchairs – conditions to make a cat feel at home. The windows were covered with wire-netting and there were two sets of wire doors with a sort of no-man's-land between them. There was a hinged trap-door at the far end, leading to a concrete and then a grass run. This open space was securely penned in with wire mesh.

Carlo escaped the very first night. I will never know how because he left no trace of his passing. He just went, and we all spent hours searching the grounds with torches. I was really very worried about the whole thing. Just on midnight, when I was thinking of giving up the search and telling Carlo's owners that their cat had got lost, the phone rang. It was none other than Carlo's mistress.

'Mr Lloyd-Jones,' she said, 'Carlo's come home. Shall I bring him back or will you come round for him in the morning?'

'In the morning,' I said wearily.

Carlo, apparently, had not only escaped, but he had made his way home unerringly, covering the five or so miles between my house and his in a shade under two hours.

I collected him the following morning, and put him back in the cattery. This was a stupid move I realise now, but at the time I thought perhaps he had sidled out while the kennel maid was inside and put it down to sheer accident. Alas, I didn't know Carlo. Two days later he was off again, in exactly the same mysterious circumstances. He just vanished overnight. We discovered his disappearance about two minutes before the phone rang.

'Mr Lloyd-Jones,' said Carlo's mistress, sweetly, 'he's come home again. Will you or shall I . . .'

This time, my blood was up. He was responding to treatment, but it would need another few days before he could officially be discharged. I put him in a large indoor cage which had once housed a monkey. One day later, the kennel maid saw Carlo lurking in the far corner of the cage. She told me afterwards: 'He looked so poor and forlorn, I thought I would give him a cuddle to cheer him up.' As she opened the cage, there was a blur of movement and Carlo left the room like a bullet, running through the house and finally leaving by way of the kitchen window. I rang his mistress immediately. 'Don't worry, he'll soon be here,' she said. 'He knows his way home by now . . .'

He did indeed. I confessed defeat, but by that time his eczema was very much better and Carlo's treatment was concluded at home.

I would dearly love to know more about the strange instinct which guided Carlo across five miles of territory he had never seen before. He took so little time to get home, he simply must have fled as straight as an arrow. He was an astonishing representative of an astonishing species.

One often hears people comparing the characteristics of cats and dogs, usually in a context that is pro one and against the other. This is rather silly, because they are entirely different animals with nothing in common except that they are four-legged mammals.

There are many recorded instances of dogs actually saving a person's life, either by warning them of impending doom, like a fire or a gas leak, or, on rarer occasions, by dragging people clear of danger. But dogs shouldn't have all the glory. I once knew of a cat which saved its owner's life.

I used to know an old lady, who has been dead now for many years, who lived on her own with only her cat for company. She was devoted to it, and used to summon me to treat it whenever it was ill. The old dear lived the life of a recluse in the bottom floor of her house. The two upper storeys had been converted into self-contained flats, and she lived, not terribly well, on the income. One day the village bobby rang me and asked me would I care for the cat while the old lady recovered from an accident in hospital. Apparently, she had insisted that he contact me before she would submit to treatment.

What had happened was this. The lady was standing on a chair to reach on the top of a huge mahogany wardrobe in her bedroom. She was very frail, and overbalanced, pulling the massive piece of furniture on top of her. And there she lay, pinned to the floor, shocked, bruised, and having great difficulty in breathing.

The cat saved her. The faithful old tabby went upstairs to the next flat and kicked up such a wailing din that the occupants guessed something was wrong. They came to the door and the cat virtually led them downstairs, where they found the old lady. They pulled the wardrobe off her and made her comfortable while they rang for an ambulance. She was taken to hospital and eventually recovered from her ordeal. I was pleased to look after the cat and made a special fuss of it. I visited the old lady while she was recovering and took the cat with me. It was deeply moving to see the fuss they made of each other. This was a wonderful medicine to help her recovery.

At the last census, it was decided that there were thirty million cats in the British Isles. I often wondered how in the world of man they could arrive at such an astronomical total, and how many cats were counted several times. But even allowing for an inaccuracy of ten per cent, that is still an awful lot of cats – far too many, certainly, for them all to be treated with kindness.

There are many people who make a living breeding cats for laboratory experiments. And many others, I feel, who make a bit on the side by stealing and snapping up strays and selling them for vivisection and experimental purposes. I would put the life of an animal equal to that of a man. I know vivisection is a complex and emotive subject. But does the quest for medical knowledge have no alternative than to subject defenceless animals to such utter cruelties, particularly without the mercy of an anaesthetic? I detest the men who torture animals in the name of science. I despise the men who turn animals into performing freaks for our entertainment. I can think of no suitable punishment for the men who deliberately introduced into England that hideous disease myxomatosis, which turned countless thousands of rabbits into something pitiful and pathetic, to be shovelled up and burned in heaps.

The turnover in animals bred for the laboratory is immense. The poor little beasts are tailor-made for the mutilating scalpel and the toxic hypodermic. Beagles are very much in demand, because they are a powerful little dog and they can absorb the sort of punishment that would kill another breed.

Years ago, I had several clients in a suburb of London and I used frequently to pass a laboratory. It was a modern, multi-storeyed building, and the appropriate department was heavily soundproofed to avoid horrifying the neighbouring residents. But often it was not enough to stop people hearing the tormented noises of the animals. I don't think it can be quite true to say they are all heavily sedated; in many cases the precise nature and location of the pain is vital to the project.

The scientific inquisition heaps some unspeakable torments on man's dumb friends. And cats, because there are so many of them, are swallowed by the laboratories in their thousands. If more people had their cats de-sexed – preferably before six months of age – it would cut down the number of unwanted and often ill-treated and hungry strays and the number of cats who find their way to the vivisection laboratory. One solution might be a cat licence, with exemptions for old age pensioners. It is tragic that just nothing is being done.

Chapter Six

HOSPITALS—AT HOME AND ABROAD

I would not like to have to reckon up just how much of my life has been spent in hospitals. I think I must hold some sort of record for hospital endurance – though I cannot compete with those poor souls who so bravely spend *all* their lives in hospital.

However, I have found it necessary to evolve my own little philosophy which governs my attitude in hospital. I would not recommend it for general consumption, but it suits me very well. For a start, I treat it simply as an extension of my normal life. I refuse to consider it as something separate and terrible. Hospital life is merely less comfortable than life at home, but for all that it sometimes has tremendous elements of humour.

The second clause which I write in to all my mental contracts with hospitals is an agreement to do just as I am told, provided the doctors tell me everything that is going on.

I think at this stage I had better explain why I have to spend so much time away from home. Polio has affected the internal plumbing and both lungs have been badly affected. So I find it very difficult to breathe, and sometimes my diaphragm just ceases to work. When this happens, lots of people dash about quite madly and I always wake up in a high, narrow and unhandsome bed. In hospital, in fact. But there is *always* someone worse off. I don't derive comfort from this, but it makes me better able to put up with my own discomforts.

The best hospital I have even been in was – and still is for that matter, because I am dictating this chapter from there – King Edward VII Hospital of Midhurst. It's an enormous building in mellow stone set near Cowdray Park in some of the most beautiful countryside. What I particularly like about the place – apart from the staff, who are absolute angels – is this rural setting. The rooms I usually occupy have big windows opening out on to a balcony and there are huge lead drainpipes up which squirrels freely climb. The birds, too, are marvellous, and I always have an improvised bird table on the parapet.

I always make good friends with the squirrels, who come into my room and actually jump on the bed. I feed them fruit and nuts, and they are particularly fond of grapes. I have often called in the squirrels to help me dispose of an embarrassment of grapes.

These squirrels nearly got me into trouble once. I was lying in bed with my head and shoulders propped up and the french windows open as usual to the balcony. It was the afternoon of the head surgeon's inspection, which was dreaded by staff and patients alike, and the rooms were polished until they shone. It was quite pleasant lying there, and I dozed off. Several squirrels then came in and helped themselves to my grapes, eating them on my bed and making a fearful mess on the covers with the skins and pips. The chief with his entourage swept in from the balcony instead of from the corridor, a bit like the General Officer Commanding with his adjutant and company. The squirrels tried to scuttle off when they saw them but were trapped in the room. There was quite a row. The sister said afterwards it looked just as if I had been eating grapes and spitting the débris out on the bed and floor.

Another incident, which I afterwards found amusing but at the time was most embarrassing, happened during another of my stays at Midhurst. One Sunday I wanted to go to the hospital's little chapel, and a male nurse was detailed to take me. The chapel is badly sited for anyone in a wheelchair: one goes down a small flight of stairs, along a well, and immediately up another flight to get there. The male nurse was not used to my wheelchair and made a great deal of noise with the manoeuvres. I was in pyjamas and dressing-gown and the chapel was strangely empty – usually there's nothing like a spell in hospital to give people an extra touch of religion. We finally made it, and I quite enjoyed what I thought was a very brief service. Then I suddenly realised that everything was set for Communion. I became a trifle worried, because I have never been confirmed and thought that I was not eligible.

Suddenly, it seemed to me, the Communion service had begun, and the reverend gentleman made a beeline towards me sitting at the back of the chapel. I expect he thought he would get me in the wheelchair done first. As he was bearing down, I whispered frantically to the nurse: 'I'm not confirmed, therefore can't take communion – you will have to take it instead.'

He whispered fiercely back: 'I'm not taking it – I'm a Seventh Day Adventist and if it wasn't for you I wouldn't be here in the first place.'

So there we were, cowering back like a couple of heathens fighting off the reverend and whispering to each other frantically. It caused such a fuss, which was exactly what I wanted to avoid. We finally fled from the chapel, kicking up an unholy din as the Seventh Day Adventist struggled with me and the chair. Later I learned from the vicar that I could have taken communion after all – it was an interdenominational service and everyone was welcome.

I have been in some strange hospitals abroad where medical facilities fell far short of the standard in this country, but the worst experience was in fact in Britain. My wretched diaphragm ran down and stopped and I collapsed. I was rushed away to hospital, and because it was such an emergency they took me to where I could have immediate treatment. A doctor got me breathing normally again and gave me an SOS injection, which is usually so large and uncomfortable it would be a considerable inducement for anyone to get up and dash home. That done, I was taken to a geriatric ward for the night.

I absolutely hated it. The staff all seemed rough and impatient and I was very conscious of the sheer hopelessness of most of the patients, who appeared to me, sadly, to be just lying there waiting to die. I know geriatric wards in this country are often overcrowded and understaffed, but I could see no excuse for the apathy and impatience.

On one side there was an elderly man dying of cancer. Across the ward was an old, old man who had been hit by a car. He was in a terminal coma and it seemed to me that life in the ward was centred on the man's rapid, shallow breathing. His mind was dead already, buried in the tomb of the faltering body. I found myself trying to follow the pattern of his breathing and then forcing myself back to my natural rhythm as I speeded up to an impossible tempo. Suddenly, the breathing stopped. The silence intruded like an explosion. And then came a corporate sigh from the other patients. It was the briefest yet most heartfelt epitaph a man ever had. I felt like crying.

It was altogether a grim and interminable night. But soon after breakfast Dorothy came, and I was never so glad to see anyone in all my life. But all I could say was: 'Thank God you're not wearing your red coat.'

'Why?' she said, thinking no doubt that I'd gone off my rocker.

'Because I'm putting on that camel coat and we're getting out of here,' I said.

So we did. I signed my release in front of a disapproving sister who looked as though she'd swallowed a bedpan, and off we went with me wearing Dorothy's nice, warm coat; but not, thank God, her red one.

Some months after the incident, a journalist wrote a terrible exposé on this particular hospital. The furore raged as high as Parliament, and I gather now that conditions have improved out of all recognition. But it really shook me. I had no idea that such hopeless, heartless wards still existed.

In considerable contrast to that place was a hospital I was once forced to enter for a few days in a town in central France. It was a mixed ward – I called it co-educational – and some of the sights that were freely displayed were sensational. But nobody seemed to care.

This arrangement was very different from another small hospital I was once taken to near Milan. I was on my way to Venice at the time, but the journey was interrupted by another bout of diaphragm-itis. I collapsed and lost consciousness. You will gather from this that travelling with me is not without its drawbacks. However, when I came to, I found myself lying, cool and peaceful, in a little stone cell. Sitting in a hard-backed chair in one corner of the room was a figure dressed in dazzling white and reading a huge book which could only have been a bible.

I thought: 'This time you've really cashed your chips and you are, against all the indications, now in heaven.'

But I hadn't. The angel in white was a nun and I was in a hospital run by a religious order. The nurses were real sisters of mercy, and I have never been nursed with more kindness in my life. It was a week before I could resume my travels to Venice.

I have always tried very hard to live with my disabilities, but once, having been given up by my English doctors as a hopeless case, I was talked into going to New York to see a world-famous consultant on respiratory ailments. It was a very expensive and not a particularly fruitful journey. The thing that created the biggest impression on me was the doctor's consulting rooms in Park Avenue – they looked just as I imagine the investiture room at Buckingham Palace, and the nurses like Miss World finalists. I was ushered into the presence of the consultant whom I sat facing across acres of stainless steel and leather desk. He looked at me piercingly and said: 'Do you sincerely want to be well enough to be able to walk up a few stairs?'

I thought this a curious opening gambit, but willingly agreed. He then gave me a thorough examination and simply told me to go back to my hotel, lie flat on my back, and have someone pile heavy books on my diaphragm and then press gently upon them. The theory was that this would get my diaphragm working of its own accord – in principle rather like priming a pump. He visited me once more, bringing with him a special belt which I had to wear round my diaphragm. He agreed that Jamaica would be a splendid place for me, and then presented me with a large bill which nearly caused a heart attack!

I must say the belt and the unconventional treatment did me a certain amount of good for a time, but it wasn't long before I was in serious trouble again.

It happened on that very visit to Jamaica which the specialist had advised and which, in fact, Dorothy, Hal and I had already planned. We had rented a house at Ocho Rios on the North Shore, and it was all just like a tropical paradise. There were yams, breadfruit and coconuts growing in the garden and the blue waters of the Caribbean lapped the golden sands a few hundred yards from the house. There was also a salt-water swimming pool in the grounds which I enjoyed very much.

It was glorious – but I was taken ill again. There was no suitable doctor, so the local doctor, a Dublin-trained coloured man who spoke with a fascinating Irish brogue, set up a little emergency centre in my room, arranging equipment and the vital oxygen cylinders.

So there I was, stuck in a stuffy villa, away from some of the most glorious sunshine in the world, breathing oxygen instead of the healthy Caribbean trade winds, with a coloured doctor kneeling at the foot of the bed reciting prayers with a Dublin accent. He told me: 'You have tried everything, your doctors have tried everything and I have tried everything. The only thing I can think of now is prayer.'

I really don't know whether or not this treatment worked, but there is an indication that it did because I'm still here! Perhaps the voodoo helped too. The staff wailed every night, thinking no doubt that I was going to die.

Two weeks later I was well enough to take a ship to Miami and then on to hospital in New York by plane. The plane was delayed for six hours by a storm, and I finally made it, after a diversion via Philadelphia. A friend had arranged for me to be met by their car and chauffeur at New York and be driven direct to the Medical Centre on the West Side. When I got there, this splendid man was still waiting, and he drove me around the city for a couple of hours until I could enter hospital at a respectable time.

Dorothy and Hal joined me a week later, travelling by ship with our luggage and oxygen cylinders. The hospital was the most luxurious hospital I have ever seen. My room (known as a River Room) had a private bath *and* shower plus a view of the George Washington Bridge and Hudson River. There were more than a thousand doctors and interns on the staff. When some Americans fall ill, they intend to suffer in style. I was at this place for five weeks, quickly losing my short-lived Jamaican tan. I underwent all sorts of tests and treatments, which only gave me very temporary relief.

If the trip so far had not had a single success, then the

journey back was a disaster. I couldn't be sure of my discharge date, and Easter was approaching, and all we could get was first-class accommodation on a small French liner. Believe me, if that was first class, I would have hated to travel steerage. I expect people there bunked in links of the anchor chain in the chain locker.

My method of embarkation was unfortunate. The tide was up, the ship was riding high and the gangway was totally unsuited for a wheelchair. As a French band piped the voyagers aboard, I boarded through an unsavoury sort of tradesmen's entrance near the bilges where the food went in and the slops came out.

The thing that caused me the biggest grief on the trip home was the lavatories. The cabins had no separate bathroom or lavatory, so it was all on a communal basis. The loos were tiny and claustrophobic, and they had automatic fans which suddenly started up and extracted air from the cubicles. These also extracted all the air from my lungs. These loos were such a curse that we devised a most involved procedure to beat the system. It was established that the ladies' lavatories were bigger and more comfortable and the extractor fans did not function with quite so much potency. So I waited until meal times and then slunk into the ladies'. Hal stood outside the door feeding me oxygen while Dorothy kept cave at the entrance. We had a couple of narrow escapes but I was never caught.

I did state earlier on in this chapter that I insisted on knowing everything the doctors were up to. So I do. The only weak link in this exercise is the attitude of the staff. Some gossip and tell all, but others are very tough nuts to crack.

The hardest person to wheedle medical information out of that I have met is a highly qualified technician at Midhurst who is liked by everyone who comes in contact with her. I was told one morning that I was going to be given an electrocardiogram check and my friend arrived with the machine and wired me up. The information on the electrocardiogram comes out on long tapes, rather like computer output. I lay back and she stood there, chatting cheerfully and 'reading' the tape as it came off the machine in yards. I watched her face like a hawk, but she carried on laughing and talking and 'reading' and I learned about as much as I would have done looking at a blank wall.

She left. Two hours later the doctor came in and asked me if I would tell him when I had had my coronary. The poker-faced minx must have seen it all on the tape, but not by word nor sign did she betray any knowledge. I have called her Poker-face ever since.

In fact, I did remember having the coronary thrombosis although I had not recognised it as such at the time. It occurred about four months previously and after feeling very poorly for a time I put it down as one of my turns.

It is very difficult not to get pensive in hospital, and although I always try to avoid introspective thinking, I sometimes ponder on the appalling responsibilities shouldered by the medical profession. Every single person in every job or profession makes mistakes, but the penalty for a medical mistake can quite easily lead to a patient's death. It's a heavy burden to shoulder – the responsibility of always being infallible.

Only once in hospital have I ever been the near victim of a mistake. I do not know whether this would have been fatal, but for reasons which I shall explain later I am quite sure it would have been most uncomfortable. I had just been admitted and was waiting for a doctor to examine me, when the door opened and a nurse backed in pulling a trolley. She looked just like a woolly monkey with a wizened little face and lots of frizzy hair. Briskly, she bared my poor old bottom and anointed it with surgical spirit. Now, I don't know if you are aware of the fact, but nurses are trained to locate the spot to be injected by drawing an imaginary cross on the buttock, and 'X' – the point of intersection – marks the spot. I could see the nurse was nervous, and assumed, correctly as it turned out, that she was brand-new. I peeped over my shoulder and saw a hypodermic containing a six cc charge – it looked as big as a stirrup-pump. I steeled myself for the prick, then nearly leaped off the bed. She had actually, physically inscribed the training cross on my backside using the tang of a file. She did this three times, and each time I nearly jumped out of my skin. It wasn't

66

painful at all, it was just that I was prepared for the dreaded needle.

Just then, providentially, the door opened and Sister walked in. She took a quick look and gently steered the nurse out. I was delighted to see the back of her who had seen so much of the back of me.

It turned out that she had made a mistake and gone to the wrong room. That massive jolt was intended for some other poor sufferer, not me! I never discovered what the injection was, but judging by the size it could very well have been for a whale.

Apart from injections and the food, one of the biggest hospital drawbacks is having a bath. Ron, who is a compact man but as strong as a horse, manages me beautifully. Not so some of the diminutive Malaysian nurses who staff our hospitals in large numbers. Don't misunderstand me. They are very kind and terribly efficient, but although they are experienced and gentle they are a bit down on muscle. I have reluctantly starred in many an aquafantasia with them on bath night.

In one incident, we all came very near to death by drowning. Two little Malaysians, looking just like twin pieces of

Dresden china, informed me that I was to have a bath and they were going to help me. I would have much preferred to wait until Ron came the following day, but almost any diversion is welcome in hospital to break the boredom, so I was led quietly off like a lamb to the sheep dip. They took me to a different bathroom, and I saw to my consternation that the sides of the bath were unusually high. Somehow, with much grunting and groaning they manoeuvred me to the rim and I flopped in like a seal from an ice floe. But there was nothing arctic about the water. It was very, very hot and I felt just like a poor old lobster. They left me there much too long, and I lay there thinking how on earth they were going to get me out. Maybe they were thinking the same thing, because they were jabbering away in their native tongue with lots of hilarious laughter. I was quite certain they were talking about me – I always am when foreigners are rattling away in my presence.

Finally, they steeled themselves for the big heave. One took my legs, the other my shoulders, and they started to lift. I was halfway up when I felt myself slipping at the back. I made a frantic grab at the nurse to the rear – and pulled her into the bath on top of me. I went right under and wondered how my lungs would react to lukewarm soapy water. She climbed out, and the proceedings became rather serious. They tried it again, and again I got off balance and almost pulled her in once more. Finally, they changed ends and managed to land me. By this time they were both at least as wet as I was. It seems funny now, and indeed we all had a laugh about it the following day. But at the time it was rather embarrassing, and from then on I have always insisted on being bathed by a male nurse or by Ron.

I will close this chapter on a note of hilarity. The incident to be described seems to me to be typical of the slapstick, mordant humour that is always close to the surface in hospital life.

It was a Saturday night many years ago, and I was in a London hospital, lying alone in a room designed for three patients. The door opened and an enormous young man was wheeled in. It seemed his entire face was in plaster, and I wondered if he had been kicked by a horse. Apparently,

it wasn't a horse but a Rugby second-row forward who probably weighed rather more. An enormous boot had felled our hero and smashed his nose and it had just been reset. To add to his troubles, the same vengeful boot had removed four teeth and opened his upper lip.

I was pondering on the brutalities of rugger when the stricken giant started to come to. He didn't mutter 'where am I' or some other traditional gambit, but started singing 'Eskimo Nell', first pianissimo and then molto forte. We got to the sad end of Dead-Eye Dick, and then he gave me a spirited rendering of 'Angeline', treble and bass.

Suddenly, he broke off, sat up in bed menacingly and demanded fruit. As it happened, I had a bowl of assorted fruit by my bedside and I took hold of an orange and summoned up enough strength to lob it over to his bed. Now, I must confess to be a failure as a thrower. I could never hit a barn door at three paces, but on this occasion I tried very hard and put my all into a spirited lob. I can still trace the horrifying trajectory of that orange. It shot out of my hand like a bullet, ricochetted off the wall and dealt him a punishing blow in the face. He bellowed like a bull and started to climb out of bed with the slow purposefulness of a man who means business. Luckily for me, his roar of anguish had alerted a nurse and she rescued me in the nick of time.

The poor man was wheeled away once more after a doctor tore off the plaster, checked to see if the nose was disturbed, and parcelled up the face once again. The following morning, the man didn't remember a thing. And I didn't bother to tell him.

Whilst concluding this book I have just heard that I am to return to yet another London hospital . . .

Chapter Seven

POLTERGEISTS–AND OTHERS

I have never seen a ghost, and I sincerely hope I never will. But I have felt one – or if it wasn't a ghost then I don't know what else it could have been. Several people well up in the world of spooks and spiritualism have told me I am psychic, and in view of some of the inexplicable things that have happened to me from time to time, I accept the proposition with very mixed feelings. One thing I am very sure – there are many things in this world of which we know little.

My first experience of the supernatural, or at least of something very much out of the ordinary, occurred during the war when I lived in a rambling old house with grounds large enough to accommodate about 160-odd dogs – all waifs, strays, evacuees or blitz victims, the bulk of whom I was looking after for their owners. We lived in the part of the house that was once the servants' quarters, for the simple reason that these were convenient and slightly more bomb-proof than the rest of the house. But I reached the stage when I would have preferred the tangible risk of high explosive to the thing that lurked on the back staircase.

I used the back stairs frequently, which were badly lit and a bit dingy, but I never sensed any presence until one day when something sensed me. I felt with horror something like a pair of hands round my neck, not choking but exerting a definite pressure. After this, it happened frequently. I used to take friends down the stairs on purpose to see what their reactions would be, and almost every time they felt this ghostly pressure round their necks. I became quite used to it, and derived a certain amount of grim amusement from other people's reactions, although I preferred to avoid that rear staircase when I was on my own – particularly at night.

After a period of time, the manifestations took a different form and for about a year, whenever I walked alone in the grounds, something would throw stones at me. I don't know whether the ghost was a bad shot because not once was I actually hit, but the missiles were definitely tangible. Sometimes the phantom thrower would continue firing as I walked indoors and many times windows were broken. It was not only frightening and tiresome, but inconvenient and expensive. Glass was hard to get during the war and I had to pull many strings to keep pace with the breakages.

I find it difficult to assess my reactions at the time – sometimes I was scared, sometimes annoyed, but it was quite a time before someone told me the house was haunted and I finally began to believe it.

Gradually, things became worse. I had always managed to get a good night's sleep because I was naturally tired after working very hard. But then the phantom started playing really weird organ music in the early hours of the morning. I was very relieved when five army officers were billeted with us, and quite delighted to learn that one of them was a padre. I wondered what effect the presence of a man of God would have on the hauntings. In fact, it made no difference whatsoever.

It was at this stage that the dogs took a hand. I always had several sleeping in my room, and they reacted strongly to the dreadful music. They always retreated to the same corner, growling with their hackles up as if the organist was actually in the room.

I told the army chaps about it at breakfast one morning and the general consensus of opinion was that I was going round the bend. However, each in turn agreed to sleep a night in my room, and there were some very thoughtful faces the following days. The padre scoffed the most, but when his turn came he slept in the room but dashed out in the small hours and insisted we changed back again. Came the morn and he, too, was a very pensive priest.

These manifestations went on and on and began seriously to upset my mother. She used to hear all sorts of noises, and pictures and ornaments would crash to the ground for no apparent reason. It was a very democratic ghost and bothered everybody in the house at various times.

On one occasion, early in the evening, I was in the grounds

milking the goats which I kept purely for the milk, which is very nutritious and was one of my ways of digging for victory, as it were. Walking back across the lawn carrying a pail of milk, I slipped and fell, spilling all the contents and twisting my ankle painfully. As I was picking myself up I heard peals of girlish laughter. I did not connect it with the ghost, thinking it was one of the kennel maids. I was very angry at her for being so heartless. But when I hobbled to the house and started to berate her, she swore it was not her. I didn't believe her at first, but later realised it just couldn't have been.

Finally, I felt this 'haunting' had gone on long enough, and, the Church of England padre having failed, contacted the village priest, a friendly man whose dog I had treated. After I had told him all about it, he said his church – he was a Roman Catholic – had a formal exorcism ceremony, and although he had never performed it, he would try to see what he could do. He walked through the house and the grounds, sprinkling holy water and making the sign of the cross and reciting prayers, and said that should help drive away the evil spirits. But it didn't help for long.

At first, things quietened down, but then it all started again with a vengeance. So in desperation, I contacted the police. What followed was pure comedy. They turned up with tin helmets camouflaged with branches and hid in the grounds around the large pond which was very deep in the middle, fringed with bulrushes, and inhabited by my Khaki Campbell ducks. At a given time I walked across the lawn and as usual was showered by the mystical stones. After three days of this they confirmed that something strange was happening and said they couldn't really help. How about calling in the CID? I thanked them for their interest, and finally took them up on the offer. They sent three men down – I called them the Ghost Squad – and they did exactly the same as their colleagues. They hid in the grounds, and I walked out with stones showering down from all directions. By this time I somehow knew that the stones would not hit me and that the thrower meant me no harm. But it was a peculiar feeling all the same.

However the CID did give me a valuable clue towards

ending the misery. They made their own inquiries within the force and advised me to contact the Marylebone Spiritualist Association. Even at that stage I wasn't entirely convinced of genuine ghosts and thought it strange that the CID, of all down-to-earth organisations, recognised the existence of spooks. I really wasn't keen to contact this organisation. I knew next to nothing about mediums and clairvoyants and did not particularly want hordes of them

stamping round the house. But as time went on and the manifestations continued I contacted the Association out of sheer desperation. What followed shook me to the core. I know it all sounds unlikely in the telling, and I know most people are as healthily sceptical as I was, but I promise you all this is true.

Two ladies arrived as arranged, on a very dark evening in the blackout, after an arduous wartime journey of train and bus. One was a very well-known medium called Estelle Roberts – I hadn't heard of her then, of course – and to my profound relief they were pleasant, kindly, ordinary people. I can't remember just what I had expected! We got down to 'business' immediately and I started to explain fully, but they told me they wanted to experience it all first hand, and could we please start in the room where the organ played its weird dirges every night with a midnight matinée sometimes. They said they would hold a séance there and, although I tried hard to get out of it, they insisted I stayed and faced the music, so to speak. I took the precaution of briefing the staff, who were all giggling fearfully and waiting for something weird to happen, and told them if I hadn't emerged within a certain time, they were to switch on all the lights and come in and get me.

We settled down in the room and first of all the women prayed and suddenly Estelle Roberts quoted a number out of the standard Church of England hymn book and recited the first and last verses of 'The Day Thou Gave Us, Lord, Is Ended'. She said this would mean something to me, and I told her it did – it was my father's favourite hymn. Then we all sat in the darkened room for a while, then she went off, or whatever one calls it, and weird voices started coming through. She said after a time she had a message for me from my father, but I was to be patient because I would not be able to understand him just yet. Frankly, I didn't think this was very likely. My father was a strange person and had been very difficult for more than a year before he died. He had not talked to me, would not see me when he was in hospital and refused to communicate with me in any way. He was a person of intense likes and dislikes, and if he didn't like a person – even his son – well, that was that. The women could not have known this, but they told me he was very unhappy and that his soul had passed away. They gave me the date of his birth and death, and were only two or three days out. Not bad when you consider they had not been told anything about him – not by me, anyway. Then they said my father was trying to come back to say how very sorry he was for being so difficult and also to thank me for looking after my mother – whom he had treated unkindly and left in a pretty bad way financially. Apparently he regretted all this and said he would do better if he had his time over again.

As further proof, the medium said, my father asked me to go upstairs and find a key hidden in one of the drawers of an old bookcase. They key would unlock another drawer, and in that I would find our old family bible. He gave me page numbers where I would find a record of family births and photographs of his mother. This, the voice had told the mediums, would prove that it really was my father speaking. I still could not – or did not want to – believe that this was my father talking, but she described him perfectly and said: 'He is taking his glasses off and pointing to a tiny mole on the side of his face.' I knew the mole well, and once as a youngster had tried to pick it off.

Suddenly, my father spoke to me directly. It was the most shattering experience of my life. The fullness of his voice was uncanny, and as he started to apologise and say he was a lost soul I *had* to believe it was him! He told me we had a loose floorboard in one of the outbuildings and that when I had had some new boards put in this had disturbed something, and that had caused the poltergeist. I immediately knew what he was talking about. One of the old outbuildings at the other side of the grounds had been converted into a kennel for some of the evacuee dogs and they had promptly started chewing the battered old floorboards. I had a hard core of grateful clients who always helped out, and they had replaced some of the floor. My father – and I cannot think who else it could have been – concluded by apologising again and told me that things would be better for me from now on. By this time I was in something of a state of shock.

But it all came to pass as he said. I found the family bible, which my mother must have locked away because she knew I had no strong affection for it. The poltergeist decided to catch up on his sleep. I couldn't help thinking what a talented and industrious poltergeist he had been – a gentle strangler, stone thrower, picture displacer and late-night organist. But it was the cessation of one of his other little tricks that caused me the most pleasure. He would constantly ring the bells on the front, back and surgery doors, causing me or the staff to dash hither and thither just in case it was a human agency. I never liked to ignore it because of emergencies and casualty cases, and, in addition, there were always families, whose lives had been disrupted by the war, begging me to look after their animals and I just didn't have the heart to say no. It was absolute bliss to hear a bell ring and *know* there would be someone there.

Estelle Roberts told me after the séance that I would be given two signs when my father was finally at peace. The first would be when a lily grew out of some water; the second would be a sign of the cross. When I saw the cross I was to keep it and then I would be protected. Despite all the shocks of that most eerie day, I still considered the signs a dubious proposition. But that winter I saw a lily growing in the centre of the lake – something completely foreign in my experience. Two weeks later I had the second sign. One night there was a very long, authoritative ring on the bell. I groaned when I heard it – it was very reminiscent of the lately departed poltergeist. I opened the door and there was no one there. It had been snowing and I saw a light shining across the porch. This in itself was strange because the blackout was in force and the only light we ever saw at night was anti-aircraft fire. But what followed was stranger still. The light was reflecting off something in the snow. It was a brass cross. And there wasn't a footprint around. As I picked up the cross the light faded.

If you think all this unlikely you have my sympathies. There was a time when I, reading something like this, would have thought the author was in need of certifying. But every word is true, and nothing would make me part with that rough little cross which meant that my poor, strange father was at peace at last. The cross is in the room with me while I am writing this.

After these experiences I hoped I was finished with the supernatural, until someone introduced me to a 'harmless little parlour game' which, for me at least, had such devastating results that I vowed never to play it again. I do not consider interfering with forces we know nothing about harmless, or a game.

You may have heard of it – one uses an upturned wineglass on a smooth table and it works on the same principle as the ouija board. The idea is to arrange the letters of the alphabet round the outside of the table with the glass in the middle. Each person present places a finger very lightly on the base of the glass, which moves apparently of its own volition, spelling out messages in exchange for questions.

The very first time we tried this we had friends in for dinner, and we thought the game would round off the evening in an amusing fashion. But right from the start it was absolutely baffling, certainly not amusing. Everyone sat around the table with their forefinger resting on the glass and someone spoke the opening phrase: 'Is there anybody there?' Almost immediately the glass started to slither wildly round the table, just as if it was examining the disposition of the letters. Finally, apparently satisfied with what it saw, it indicated 'yes'. During this period I had the strangest feeling. The hair on my neck was rising and falling exactly like the hackles of a dog and I had a powerful feeling that something strange was with us in the room. Frankly, I would have been quite happy to have called the whole thing off. The 'spirit' or whatever it was was asked its name and it spelled it out. It was a French name. And gradually, under our questions, the following story emerged.

The man was a radio operator in the Merchant Navy. He had been killed in a torpedo sinking when on a tanker on a Liverpool to Murmansk convoy in 1942. He described the start of the convoy, the Royal Navy escort ships, and the frequent attacks from German submarines and aircraft. He gave the names of the escorts and described how one of them had been torpedoed and sunk. As this extraordinary story proceeded I got someone to take notes – I was determined to check the authenticity of the communication.

Eventually, we ended the game by thanking the 'voice' and signed off for the night. Several days later I contacted a journalist friend of mine and asked how we could check this information. He thought for a bit, and then said he would ring me back. The following day he came round to see me. He was very much a matter-of-fact person but was obviously shaken. 'Buster,' he said, 'I spun the Royal Navy records department a yarn and they agreed to check the information from their files . . .' he paused for effect '. . . and every single detail you gave me was true.'

Naturally he wanted to write a story about 'local author's sensational séance' or something, but I asked him not to. Many people would have looked upon this as absolute confirmation of my crankiness and the whole thing sounds so unlikely. But I consider it equally unlikely that anyone will ever give me a rational explanation of the incident.

I have only played this 'game' twice more. The first time we had a very lively conversation with a woman called Hilary, who said she had been drowned while swimming in Norfolk in 1954. Hilary was a very cheerful person, and kept telling us that 'everything was going to be all right'. I couldn't decide whether she meant immediately or ultimately, when we too would just be vibrations spelling out messages through a glass.

The last time was just before my most recent spell in hospital. After a French sailor and the cheery Hilary, I was wondering which type of spirit we would get that night. As it happened, we got my father.

He told me I was going into hospital (more than a day before my doctor decided the same) and he added that I was going to be all right. Then he asked me to contact him again when I came home, using the same method. He was perfectly correct about going into hospital, and he was right about me coming home, although I think there was a time when a couple of leading chest specialists might have disagreed with him. As for what else he wanted to tell me, I shall never know. As I said earlier, there are some things in which I feel it unwise to dabble and this is one of them. I have no wish to participate in the 'wineglass game' again.

These experiences, bewildering as they were, have left me much to think about the supernatural – so called only because we do not understand it. I was just as sceptical when I was introduced to what people call faith healing, although I am very sure that *all* healing contains elements of faith – a surgeon's faith in his skill, a person's faith in his doctor; the very will to get better is an act of faith.

However, it all started more than twelve years ago when I really was very ill. I was in a London chest hospital, unconscious much of the time, and I am quite sure some of the doctors had just about given me up. I didn't have to be clairvoyant to gather this. I had apparently become unconscious while undergoing an internal chest examination which necessitates swallowing yards of tubing, when I heard the doctor say quite clearly: 'I'm afraid he's in a bad way, both his lungs are septic.'

It's a funny thing about some doctors. They will rarely tell you anything when you want to know, but can be awfully frank when they think you can't hear them. I often wished this particular chap had been a bit more careful that day. The fact that I had septic lungs hasn't, to put it mildly, helped me on and off for twelve years. I would definitely have preferred not to hear that particular piece of information.

Another unpleasant thing about this hospital was the room in which they stuck me. I needed to have bags of oxygen, and the room was directly downwind from the huge hospital chimney. I hate to think what they were burning, but it belched a particularly foul brand of smoke and soot straight into my room. Just the thing, I thought, for my septic lungs! I often thought that this hospital did me more harm than good. I 'created' with as much strength as I could muster and finally was moved to another room upwind from that wretched chimney.

One compensation of the period was a sister who tended me. She was a most wonderful woman, gentle, compassionate and a credit to her calling. Once, on her precious day off, she went to church to pray for me and then came back to see how I was. She had seen much pain and suffering, but had not lost the capacity to be moved by it. The strange thing was that when we first began to know each other, we didn't get on well at all. I thought she was a hard-boiled tyrant, and goodness only knows what she thought of me. It just shows how misleading first impressions often are.

Eventually, the specialist thought there was nothing more he could do for me – in my time I must have been a major undermining influence on the morale of the medical profession – and he packed me off home, heavily laden with powerful antibiotics and strict instructions to take them regularly in large quantities. Among the drugs I had to take was cortisone, which in those days was still something of an unknown quantity.

While in hospital I met Dorothy Evans, a physiotherapist and a most remarkable woman. After leaving the hospital, she used to come down in her own time to treat me, always after a hard day's work. Her objective was to help me breathe in the right way, and I shall always be grateful to Miss Evans for the help she gave me.

A considerable source of grief to me in those days was the fact that I could not convalesce at Denes Close. I really was in a sorry state, and it was considered that all the animals and bustle at home would not do me any good. In retrospect I think it would have done me all the good in the world, but anyway I took up residence in an hotel suite and slowly fought my way back to moderate health.

In those days I was still far from reconciled to my condition and ever hopeful that someone, somewhere, would be able to put me on the road to recovery; and out of the blue that someone appeared.

My first faith healer just arrived unannounced and said he was going to visit me three afternoons a week. And did I mind? I said no, but doubted whether I could afford his services. I was astonished when he told me he did not work for money. He was a fascinating man. Apparently he had owned a wine-importing business in India, but this went dry on him and he went into the antique business. Then suddenly he had a revelation – he felt the urge to help sick people and was full of an inner conviction that he could. He trained and prepared for his healing for five long years and went about it with astonishing dedication. During this time, of course, he was not able to remain in business, so his urge to help heal cost him much in material things.

This dedicated man helped me over many bad attacks. In fact, we alternated between him and my regular doctor, and I lived in dread of something happening and them both turning up together. I expect you know how the medical profession generally reacts to faith healing. It's a bit like waving a red rag at a bull.

One day I passed out completely, and my household were so concerned that they sought double insurance and called both doctor and healer. I remember coming to and seeing one at one side of the bed and the other sitting opposite. To my absolute joy they got on splendidly together and my fears were groundless. Both the healer and my doctor helped me a lot and the latter was and is very much a personal friend.

I think the healer's greatest contribution to my general state of health was directed at my own mental approach. He made me think about things in quite a different way. I ceased to dwell on my disabilities and concentrated more on the pleasanter things. I became vividly aware of life as a series of experiences and took a delight in the tiny things – the dawn chorus of birds outside the window, the feel of a clean pair of sheets; all the little things that had previously paled to insignificance beside the spectre of my illness. When I was in pain, I accepted it and looked forward to the time when it would stop. This made it something positive, instead of just a torment. It was by way of being permanent therapy, and I can honestly say that this man had a profound effect on my life.

Another thing he taught me was the power of prayer. I am not, frankly, a religious person in the accepted sense of the word, and perhaps the God I pray to is not the thundering Jehovah of the Old Testament, but I have always found that prayer does work. The more I think about it the more I realise that faith is the most potent natural power of all.

Sadly, my very good friend the faith healer fell ill himself and was taken to a nursing home, needing constant attention. It was tragic irony that this man who had helped so many people needed help himself. Happily (but I was sad to lose a friend) he passed away in September 1971.

I might appear a little dense, but it wasn't until I had been at the receiving end of faith healing that I began slowly to realise how much of it I had unconsciously practised in my work with animals. Only I didn't call it faith; if I had sat down and thought about it, I would have described it, perhaps, as intuition or a gift. The same thing, if you examine the proposition.

I began to get a reputation where 'hopeless' cases were concerned. The word quickly spread and I received animals quite literally from all over the country. I was never very happy at this state of affairs – it meant for a lot of the time I was treating rank outsiders which other people clearly thought would never stay the course. In ninety per cent of these cases the owners had been to conventional vets and their pets had been treated with drugs and injections and they just had not worked. I always worked with natural materials and know with absolute certainty that herbs and natural feeling techniques achieved cures in cases where everything else had failed.

But for all that, there were many cases where I found myself baffled. I used to feel very depressed, and the responsibility weighed heavily upon me. When I found myself in a situation like this I would pray in a simple way: 'Oh dear God, show me the way, show me how to cure this animal.' Often after prayer I would run my hands over the dog and form a definite impression of what was wrong and what was needed to cure him. And sometimes I would just sit down and dictate a complete diet and treatment to my secretary without quite knowing why I was doing it. The words would just flow out exactly as if I was a medium tapping some unearthly source of knowledge. I can take no credit for this, it was something completely out of my hands.

There were failures but it was wonderful to see really sick dogs responding to treatment. You could see their coats getting better, their eyes getting brighter. I tried always to thank God for the help I had been given to cure them.

People used to come to my surgery waiting-room from miles away without an appointment and wait hours, if necessary, for me to see their pets. All they wanted me to do was the mystic 'laying on of hands'. It used to make me feel so embarrassed and hypocritical, but what could I do? It obviously meant so much to them and it was not a difficult task.

I realised that it would be easy to delude myself that it was always as easy as that, and would work twice as hard to cure animals in my usual way. I felt deep down that my alleged 'powers' should not be used lightly. All in all, I found this period a most strenuous time and often felt as wrung out as an old dishcloth. I think one could say that my practice was founded on faith or hope, cemented with a lot of very arduous physical work.

Everyone who worked with me sensed the help that faith was giving me. It went on and on and my practice got bigger and bigger and I reached the miserable state of having to refuse to treat sick animals. I was overworking frantically and my health, always poised on a knife edge, began to break down again. I badly needed a complete rest.

Finally, I broke down. I spent more than three months in bed and had another miserable period in hospital. When I got back home I felt very weak and very ill and I just knew that whatever powers I had had been all used up. I was drained and exhausted. A few appointments were made in an attempt to coax some interest back, but it was no use. It was just as if a light had been turned off. I think that that particular bout had finished all the goodness and healing that was transmitted through me – perhaps I had unconsciously absorbed it all in the struggle to stay alive. I don't know, but to this day I have never been able to treat another animal in this way.

It was all brought home to me very poignantly when General Tollemache, who is now Sir Humphrey Tollemache, an old and valued client, persuaded me to look at his favourite springer spaniel, a much loved old dog called Bob. He put Bob on the table and asked me a couple of simple questions, but I could not have answered him if my life depended on it. It was a terrible blow.

Time passed slowly and then I started a rather unpleasant time. I was in a wheelchair in dreadful pain from a paralysed arm, and I really wondered if life was worth the living. I had pain-killing drugs which threw me into deep depression, and then my specialist decided I would have to have the nerve severed in my bad arm. This was almost as drastic a step as amputation, because it meant that the arm would be completely useless for ever.

It was then I began to get a grip on myself. I thought of my old healer, and derived much comfort from remembering again what he had said. He was too ill himself to help, but I thought of other healers, and remembered someone had given me the name of one who lived barely five minutes away from home.

This was another changing-point of my life. I phoned for an appointment at the Lawson Rhodes Foundation and saw the healer later that week. He looked at my arm and said there was no reason why it should not get better. And this, remember, was just after a notable specialist had said that drastic surgery was the only remedy. There was a time when I would have scoffed, but having acquired knowledge and humility the hard way, I had faith in his healing. After a long chat, he asked me to come back and see him again in two weeks' time. I couldn't wait to get back and, when I did, he had some 'helpers' with him and they worked on my arm. They did nothing in the medical sense – they just felt along it gently. The effect was almost miraculous. The pain started to disappear and after several visits, I needed neither a sling nor pain-killing drugs for that arm. I can now raise the arm above shoulder level. Before that it was almost completely paralysed and a singularly useless append-age. I often go cold when I think how nearly I lost faith and was almost reconciled to surgery which would have denied me any use of that arm for the rest of my life.

I think the most remarkable faith healer I ever met was a Brazilian. I first met him in 1968 when he came to see me, having read my first book. Apparently, he had decided he could help me, and help me he certainly did.

At our first meeting he came with three helpers and they 'operated' on my other arm – the right one – and in no time at all the partial paralysis had almost disappeared. I was absolutely overjoyed and full of expectations when he told me he would see me again later that week. He said he had to go to treat someone in Belgium, and would return with some herbs that would help me. He returned with the herbs and we arranged another healing session. Meanwhile, he asked me to invite fifty or sixty people to the session to help him by giving prayer and thoughts. I remember think-ing it had all the ingredients of a super party. However, he turned up at the appointed time and found me and fifty-odd people waiting.

The Brazilian asked me if he could use the kitchen, and proceeded to brew up a very smelly potion, using his herbs with a base of some sort of fat. Then he had the bath filled with hot water and asked me to get in along with generous dollops of his brew. My right leg had been paralysed for a long time and I had very little feeling in my left leg. He started to massage them in the bath, adding more hot water from time to time. I felt anxious, and hopeful, and very humble when I thought of all those people in the other room praying and thinking about us. After a while I had a feeling like tiny electric shocks running through both my legs. They started tingling, and gradually I could feel him touching my right leg. It was a strange sensation because I had felt nothing there for a long time. It became very sensitive, and finally I could feel everything. Then he started on my left leg. He massaged and massaged, and after about half an hour I had a very faint feeling in my toes. The sensation slowly spread along the foot and up my leg. At this stage he became quite excited and called in three of his helpers. The session terminated by my being able to stand on my own for the first time in years. I even managed three tentative, tottering steps. It seemed to me to be a miracle.

But clearly the Brazilian was just getting warmed up. One of the people in the main party was a woman who had a small growth inside her eyelid which doctors had said was inoperable – apparently it was in such a bad place they considered it best left alone. Anyway, he asked for some scissors, and asked her to lie down on a settee while I held her hand. And with no anaesthetic or anything he started snipping the growth off. I was frankly petrified. I whispered to her: 'Is it awful, is it agony?'

She laughed. 'It doesn't hurt a bit. In fact, I am amused because you look so fearful. You are the one suffering, not me,' she said.

As it happened, she was perfectly correct. He snipped the thing away and there was no blood and no trouble at all. How does one explain a thing like that?

There was to be more healing on that incredible day. Denise Robins was one of the group. She was wearing a plaster corset and a cast round her neck and was in terrible pain. At that time she was suffering from arthritis and the only thing to ease the pain was the support given by the plaster. Denise was clearly very nervous. The Brazilian undid the corset very gently and started moving his hands over her back but not touching her. He was praying at the same time.

After about ten minutes he began very gently to massage her back, and gradually did so quite vigorously. Denise was laughing and then crying with gratitude and relief and finished up by jumping off the bed and kissing us both, which was all very gratifying.

Shortly afterwards, he left the country to heal in other parts of the world, and I don't think he has returned to England. I wish he would – I've got a few more jobs for him! Seriously though, he is a most remarkable man and I count myself fortunate to have met him. I have heard from other people that he is treated like a saint in his native Brazil and once cured the president of the country of heart trouble. This, more than anything else, gave him some official recognition, because faith healing is frowned upon by the medical profession in Brazil just as it is in this country. I really don't know why. If a man is sincere about it, I can see no reason why a faith healer shouldn't try where the doctors have failed. I suppose the subject is a fertile field for charlatans and the authorities cannot control things like experience and qualifications. They do like a mass of certificates to establish a man's bona fides.

The Brazilian, incidentally, flatly refused to take money. He travels round the world healing, helped by a fund which was established for him by many grateful supporters in Brazil.

I do hope I haven't given a false impression with all this. I would be the last man to criticise the medical profession – but for a number of surgeons and doctors and nurses, I am sure I wouldn't be here – but healers have given me a great deal of comfort and help in the past, and it would be very wrong of me not to acknowledge it.

Generally I find people who scoff and call faith healing a lot of nonsense are healthy – it is only when in pain and sickness and when conventional treatments fail that such people look elsewhere and consider any alternative.

Chapter Eight

SEEKING A HOBBY

In my quest to find the perfect hobby, one which would dovetail neatly in with my disabilities and provide me with the sort of interest that stops one turning introspective, I have tried everything from painting to keeping tropical fish. And rarely can anyone have failed so completely at so many has grown from practically nothing to the finest sucking loach fish, called Hoover because he is a scavenger and keeps the tank clean. Despite all my ham-fisted ministrations, Hoover has grown from practically nothing to the finest sucking loath this side of the Ganges. He is currently six inches long and is growing steadily.

There was a time when I didn't need a hobby. My work was my life, and my main outside enjoyment was driving my convertible sports car at what, in retrospect, seems to be a breakneck speed. And I was always interested in art and a frequent visitor to the famous galleries in London, Paris and Rome. Apart from just viewing, I started dabbling actively in art during my regular visits to my Paris practice. Gradually I became friendly with a few artists, most of whom were usually penniless and literally starving; indeed, the Goddess of Art is a hard mistress.

I felt so sorry for them, starving most unromantically in the traditional Parisian garret, that I used to buy some of their work. It was not entirely a charitable exercise: I suppose I always hoped at the back of my mind to own a painting that would one day be worth thousands as a perfect example of the early work of so-and-so. But it was not to be, and to my knowledge none of those poor, poverty-stricken artists has ever become rich and famous.

I did meet some unforgettable characters however. The most impressive in every sense was a man who owned a gorgeous gourmet restaurant in St Cloud. He weighed twenty-six stone and his hobby, apart from eating, was art. He ran a permanent exhibition of paintings in rooms over his restaurant – including more than two hundred portraits, all of him, painted by artists in exchange for food. To be accepted to the group, an artist had to show promise by painting a passable portrait of the proprietor. If accepted, the artist could then paint his own subjects which were hung in another room for sale. If the restaurateur met an artist whose work was particularly impressive, he would sponsor him to the tune of bed and board. He had a permanent but ever changing little colony, and the members fed very well from the kitchen left-overs. Some of the work, of course, was not good, but many of the paintings soared in value and his private collection is by now worth a great deal of money. I could never work out whether he was a benefactor or a speculator.

From time to time, this overweight aficionado of the arts would sell some of the work, and he had one painting which positively haunted me. It was by a man called Selim, who has since become very famous but was at one time as hungry as his impoverished colleagues. It was an impressionist study which meant different things to different people, but I always saw in the riot of images and colours what appeared to me to be Christ's head under water. This painting was for sale, but for some reason I didn't buy it. When I returned home I wished I had, and I used to dream about it.

A few weeks later, I went back to St Cloud specifically to buy the Selim. But when I got there I found to my profound disappointment that the painting had just been sold. I felt really desolate, and all I could think to do was to take the buyer's name and address. It took me several days to pluck up the courage to see the new owner, but I finally did. It was a woman, and she had a most beautiful home, happily for me near Paris, with a gorgeous salon practically covered in splendid paintings. I told her how much I had admired the Selim and she was very sympathetic, letting me in to see it once more. We stood there looking at it. Once again I saw clearly Christ's head under water. I told her and she clapped her hands and 'ooh-la-la-la-ed'. Apparently both she and her husband saw exactly the same thing.

I left sadly, but the image still haunted me. Just before I returned to England I telephoned her, and she agreed to let me take one last look at it. She must have realised, bless her, just what it meant to me, because as we were gazing at it she said, suddenly: 'You poor man. Fancy going back to England without a bit of French colour. I will sell it to you for the money I paid.' The price was fortunately within my means so I was absolutely overjoyed. I bore the Selim off in triumph and gratitude back to London, and one of the first people to see it in my surgery was Lady Norton, the collector and expert in art. She identified it immediately as a Selim, and told me she was going to France very shortly and hoped to visit his studio.

The painting was much admired and occupied pride of place until I moved to The Penthouse. It was heartbreaking but it didn't seem to fit in anywhere. I tried it in every room in the place, but somehow the magic was gone. So I sold it to Lady Norton, on the understanding that she would sell it back to me when I wanted it. It could well fit in with my present home at Denesland, but to date I haven't had the courage to ask for it back.

My own personal artistic appreciation was helped along by Mary Kessell, the famous modern artist. She was commissioned by the War Artists' Advisory Committee and became the first woman artist to be allowed to work in Belsen, the Nazi concentration camp, immediately after the war. Poor Mary had a tough time there, and her horror was reflected in her work. Some of her drawings of the inmates are the most haunting things, and I know it took her years to recover from the distress caused by the things she saw. Mary, in her search for authenticity, also spent two solid weeks at Berlin Station, watching and drawing as thousands of people literally strapped themselves to the outside of trains in their urgency to flee the city. Again, the pity and hopelessness of the situation came through magically in her work.

Mary, of course, was exhibited at the Tate, and she took me several times to the soirées there. These are to art what Glyndebourne is to opera, and it was an unforgettable experience to see the Tate lit entirely by candles, tiny pinpoints of brilliance flickering like diamonds in the fantastic chandeliers. The paintings seemed to glow with a life of their own and it was all very, very beautiful.

I first met Mary in 1940 when she came to see me in the haunted house at Feltham with a dachshund which was suffering from back trouble. It was the start of a strong friendship, and she taught me all I know about artistic appreciation. But one thing she couldn't teach me was how to paint. I fear that no one could. She started me off, and I even took formal lessons, but a child with a tarbrush and a bucket of creosote could have bettered my finer efforts.

Naturally, being me, I tried to run before I could walk. I bought everything an artist should have, including an easel. I swiftly dismissed water colours as being far too elementary for a budding genius and got stuck straight into oils. And I mean stuck. I think my face used to attract paint like a magnet and I used to have more of it on me than the palette.

Then the strain of painting would affect my arms, but I was not able just to leave off. The expensive, camelhair brushes had to be cleaned; so did the palette. By the time I had packed up, I didn't have the strength to clean myself. I used to hate asking people to clean my hands with turps, and detest having to lie in bed for the rest of the day because I had used up all the oxygen in my muscles.

In fact, it was very disappointing but I just had to hang up my palette and retire. I had found painting to be absolutely fascinating and was making a certain amount of progress, but it was to no avail. I took up drawing as the next best thing, but again my muscles rebelled and I had to give that up too.

I can't tell you how much I admire those splendid people who learn to paint with their feet and teeth, overcoming all kinds of dreadful disabilities to do so. I was given a beautiful calendar once, painted by spastics and people with no arms. It must be a truly wonderful thing to see people rise above their grievous handicaps and fulfil themselves by painting.

At the other end of the scale, I once spent a day at the home of Henry McIlehenny, a vastly wealthy man whose grandfather endowed the huge museum and art gallery in Philadelphia. But not even Mr McIlehenny could afford the fantastic insurance on the army of old masters which hung in ranks across the wall of his palatial home. He 'borrowed' them, in fact, in rotation from the gallery. It was an unforgettable if not a very relaxing experience, because the whole house was bristling with armed guards. I suppose it had to be, because the contents were literally worth millions.

However, having reluctantly decided that painting was not for me, I cast round for something else to do. I thought I had found the answer when an actor friend of mine introduced me to a portable celestial telescope – an enormous thing about six feet long – which I suspect he was trying to sell me. I had it for a time at The Penthouse, which already enjoyed some of the finest views on the south coast.

At first, it was absolutely marvellous. I could see the moon in full detail, stars I didn't know existed, and during the day people fishing from the West Pier. Three miles away to the east, I could see the noble stretch of Lewes Crescent, where so many of my friends lived. It was almost equally fascinating to watch the ships at sea and quite clearly see the sailors going about their duties.

But there was a snag. In this case it took a lot of physical effort to focus and adjust the huge telescope and I couldn't manage it myself. I had just decided reluctantly to part with it when my actor friend crystallised my suspicions and offered it to me for a sum which was as astronomic as its subject's function. So the telescope returned from whence it came, and I had to revert to the more modest performance of the naked eye.

My next hobby was photography. I was deeply appreciative of the views from The Penthouse and liked nothing better than to sit in what we called the Winter Garden, snug and warm, watching storms crashing huge waves against the groynes. Surely it would be a simple matter, I thought, to record all this on film.

I was pushed into Brighton to a big camera shop, and the manager, who was most helpful, showed me dozens of the latest cameras, most of which were made in Japan, with built-in exposure meters and automatic everything, so simple that a child could produce first-class work. Good for junior; but I certainly couldn't.

The manager came up in his own time and spent hours trying to teach me to take photographs. I spent a fortune, but practically nothing came out. I would take a portrait shot, get the shakes and miss the subject completely, although the background would be superb. I would snap a racing yacht heeling over close inshore and only get the sea. It was all very frustrating. I had the artistic appreciation to be a good photographer; my art studies had taught me about composition and effective background, but my practical performances were deplorable. I realised I would never be a Karsh, and retired from photography while I had a little money left.

I think I only took one good photograph during my exposure to cameras, and that, almost miraculously, was of the Queen. She was making a whistle-stop tour of Sussex, and one of her halts was at the Searchlight Cripples' Home at Seaford, an occasion to which I was invited because we were interested in helping that very worthwhile charity. I was sitting in my wheelchair, hands holding a loaded camera more in hope than anything, when the Queen came within range. I became all emotional and my hands were trembling like leaves in a gale. The Queen, God bless her, noticed that I was in difficulties, and asked me: 'Have you taken it?'

I stammered: 'No,' and that radiant and incredible woman, in the middle of a tour so hurried and hectic that it would have exhausted a strong man, stood waiting patiently while I pulled myself together and took a couple of snaps. It seems like a fairy-tale ending, and the picture matched the occasion – it came out beautifully, a lovely informal-looking shot, which is now one of my treasured possessions.

After this, I started to dabble in bridge. Dorothy, of course, was an international player and is still absolutely red hot. She offered to teach me, and I could not have hoped for a more expert tutor, but I refused because it would have been very boring for her. But I did read a book on the game with little or no comprehension, and strongly suspected that the intricacies of bridge would be as unfathomable as photography.

And so it transpired. I had a teacher, but after a few

lessons I knew I would never make a player. The thought of playing with Dorothy, who can remember a hand literally years afterwards, was ridiculous – I could never remember what I had just put down. So I took up backgammon, which is now my favourite game.

One great source of consolation to me during this frustrating period of trying and failing to find a hobby was Puddy, my beloved pug. He came everywhere with me, and particularly loved my wheelchair. The only time he ever left me on a walk was to go and sniff another wheelchair; I think he wanted to see whether it was the same species.

Looking after Puddy, in fact, took up as much time as any hobby. Pugs have lots of places and creases on their faces which have to be cleaned regularly. Pud had a nasty sore place on his nose which required regular attention. His teeth weren't very good and needed a daily clean, and so did his ears. It was quite a job, and I remember not being able to have my own bath until I had groomed Puddy. This brought home to me very sadly just how much I had deteriorated physically. There was a time when I used to attend to sixty or seventy dogs a day, many of them big ones, but frequently I had to take a rest in the middle of grooming a patient little pug.

One thing I desperately desired at this stage of my life was independence. I have always been a great one for doing my own thing, and I sometimes got to the stage when I thought I would scream if I couldn't get away on my own for a couple of hours. You can imagine my joy, then, when Dorothy gave me a surprise birthday present – an electric wheelchair, fully road-going with number-plates and a tax disc and everything. I think people tended to worry about me when I was out in it – with good cause, as you will see later – but I personally was overjoyed. I felt like a child with his first cycle, and the wheelchair greatly extended the boundaries of my own little world.

It was the most wonderful thing to sally forth on my own with nobody having to push me and only the faithful Puddy to keep me company. I revelled in my new-found freedom, and certainly Puddy heartily approved – he always liked to have me completely to himself. Frequently Puddy and I would have little set-tos with silly ladies. They would see Puddy trotting along by my side and have the cheek to accuse me of ill-treating him! 'That poor little dog, he's worn out, he's exhausted,' they would say. 'You are a very cruel man and I shall report you to the RSPCA.' Sometimes a lady fiercer than the others would physically stop my gallop by holding up my wheelchair with her stick or sunshade. I used to get so angry at the silly old trouts. They just didn't have the sense to see that Puddy was panting with excitement and with the absolute joy of life and that he was nowhere near exhausted.

Actually, my biggest problem was keeping up with Puddy, because he was a very athletic little dog and my wheelchair went very slowly. But even now I still feel a little bitter about these interfering old busybodies. I wonder how many other people are going through the same experience as me.

Puddy and I had many adventures with my wheelchair. There was the time I broke all the regulations governing my journeys and determined one afternoon that Puddy and I would travel to Rottingdean by way of the Undercliff Walk, which starts at Black Rock, itself a long way from Hove, in a battery-powered wheelchair. I suppose the total round trip would have been ten or twelve miles, an impossible epic under the circumstances.

However, off we set, me well wrapped up against the coldish wind and Puddy on my lap when he decided he'd walked far enough. I know it doesn't sound much in the telling, but to me it was a great adventure – I had never ventured any further than between the piers. It was absolute bliss to be travelling slowly along the Undercliff Walk, with the great white bulk of the cliff on one side and the glorious sweep of the sea on the other. And, I am proud to say, Puddy and I made it to Rottingdean before the inevitable happened and the batteries ran out of juice. It wasn't long before my exhilaration turned to depression. The chilly wind suddenly became an icy blast, and the bright afternoon turned to early dusk. We sat there on the lonely walk feeling more forlorn as the time went by. Finally, and luckily, a

couple came along. I explained the position and they started a rescue operation. Pud and I were taken home, and the wheelchair was picked up in a van and taken off to have its batteries charged. And I was in disgrace back at The Penthouse for going absent without leave and causing everyone a lot of worry.

This was one of the faults with the wheelchair. Its endurance was governed by the life of the batteries, which was extremely limited. And when I ran out of power, which I did quite often, it caused a lot of problems getting me back and the chair was too heavy to be pushed back home by a single person. Rescue parties were necessary, and when this happened my feelings of independence quickly evaporated in the harsh light of reality. In the end I used to get quite neurotic about the state of charge of the batteries and watched them as though my life depended upon them. But it was a great joy to me to get out on my own and watch Puddy dashing about enjoying himself, revelling in the extra mobility. He absolutely adored the seafront, and when we moved a mile further inland to Denesland I am sure he blamed me. Certainly he has never appeared to be as fond of me as he used to.

One occupation which used to give us both a great deal of pleasure was feeding the Hove seagulls. Working on the premise that seagulls are always hungry and that the exercise would do me good, I would always leave The Penthouse with a big bag of bread and throw pieces to the birds. It was marvellous to see the gulls swoop down with superb aerobatics and catch the bread in mid-air. Puddy was delighted by their performances, but never barked or made a fuss.

The gulls loved it too, but I was completely wrong about the exercise bit. I may well have overdone it, but the strain of throwing bread in the air began to exhaust me, and there came one awful day when I couldn't move my arms at all. I was absolutely exhausted and I couldn't move them an inch. I asked a passerby if he would help, and he walked all the way to The Penthouse to get aid. Along came yet another rescue party and I was pushed back home and the wheelchair to the garage. I realised then that even tossing bread to the gulls was too difficult a task for me.

My glorious days of semi-independence came to an abrupt halt one day when I was proceeding along Hove seafront absolutely flat out with Puddy sitting in my lap loftily surveying the passing world. Suddenly the chair hit a huge rock, crashed out of control, and overturned. The chair was a write-off, I was bruised and shaken up, but Paddy was completely unhurt.

All in all, it wasn't as serious an accident as it might have been, but I considered the writing was on the wall. I was unable to control the wheelchair as well as I used to, and it would have endangered other people as well as myself if I had carried on. I had to give it up, and it made me sad and depressed for ages – particularly on those fine spring mornings when the sea sparkled and the air crackled with ozone and I wanted nothing more than to go out; just Puddy and me.

So it was back to the push-chair, which took a lot of getting used to again. My male nurse at that time had a deep-rooted objection to exercising himself, which meant a minor battle every time Puddy and I wanted exercising. You can imagine how unpleasant it was after months of going it alone.

One thing I have had more than a passing interest in for years is tropical fish. I'd always admired them in waiting rooms and surgeries and found the bright colours in amongst the soft greens of the plants and gravels had a strong therapeutic effect. So I decided to become a breeder. I accumulated large tanks, small tanks and nursery tanks and, indeed, sometimes the occupants would breed. But again, I found it very hard work chasing fish with a tiny net and it was all a great strain on my arms.

I thought at first that my natural aptitude with animals would help me with the fish, which just goes to show what an incurable optimist I am. It was no help at all, of course, because guppies and things think all men look alike.

Being very green at first I made the beginner's classic mistake of putting small fish in with a nasty big one and then wondering where half the tiddlers had disappeared to overnight. I still have a tank with a few fish but, as I said at the start of this chapter, my only notable success has been Hoover. He must be the Gaylord Hauser of the fish world, and if it wasn't for him my reputation as an aquarist would be near zero.

I suppose my lack of success at hobbies helped me to turn to writing, although it is far too strenuous to be termed a hobby. I mean strenuous mentally; it's quite easy physically and one does not have to be able to write at all, if you see what I mean. I plan the structure of a book first and then dictate all my thoughts on to a tape-recorder dealing with one chapter at a time. By the time the tapes have been transcribed a pattern usually begins to emerge. Several polishing sessions and I have the finished article, without once putting pen to paper. Thank God I can still talk!

I find writing a book a little like a mountaineer must feel when he's climbing a new peak. The first few chapters are the foothills and are negotiated quite easily. Then things get steeper and the effort becomes progressively more intense. The last few thousand words appear like an unattainable summit, to be glimpsed but not reached.

Actually, it's my own silly fault. When I look back I could kick myself for wasting so many opportunities to learn about writing. Many of my clients were famous and prolific authors, including Fleur Cowles, Denise Robins, Ursula Bloom, Jane Lane, the historian, and Flora Sandstrom. Other friends, alas now dead, were Naomi Jacobs, Louis Golding, Godfrey Winn and Dennis Mackail. Fancy missing a spot of literary tuition from that galaxy of talent.

And they really were friends of mine. All of them, with the exception of Fleur Cowles, either wrote a book about me, a chapter on me or dedicated a book to me. This is a fact of which I am very proud.

Chapter Nine

ARE YOU A DOG LOVER?

It really is very difficult. Here am I all set to answer at a swoop literally hundreds of letters about how to choose a puppy, when I know with absolute certainty that it is the puppy who will choose *you*.

They can afford to be selective, too. There are only some four million dogs in this country and about fifteen times that number of humans, so the competition is intense. However, in all modesty, I can say I have always done well. Many are the pups in search of a master, or strays in search of a meal ticket, who have adopted me over the years. These have spanned the whole, rich spectrum of dogs, from lordly pedigrees whose parents practically lived at Crufts, down to hell-raising mongrels conceived and born on the other side of the tracks, probably under the most astonishing circumstances.

One dog I will never forget was Paddy. Paddy was the result of a most unlikely bout of miscegenation involving, certainly, a foxhound and a boxer, with probably a touch of Airedale and a smattering of samoyed not too far in the background. Paddy was a prodigious breeder and a knock-down, drag-out fighter who would have taken on a Royal Bengal tiger just for the hell of it.

Paddy decided to adopt me one day just outside Lamberhurst in rural Kent. It was a beautiful day, and we pulled up on the verge to enjoy a good whiff of the Kentish air. Suddenly, Paddy appeared. He was proceeding along a ditch in bloodhound fashion with his nose cleaving a furrow in some rich, agricultural mud. He was absolutely plastered in it and smelled like a farm-yard. He looked, saw me, and came forward very warily. He eventually allowed himself to be patted and I remembered thinking that he had been ill-treated – his wariness was obviously compounded with fear. I rubbed his ears and talked to him gently, then I patted his back. He yelped in agony, and when I looked closer I saw blood among the mud matting his coat. He was also very thin. He wore no collar, of course – I later discovered that getting Paddy to wear a collar was like persuading Cassius Clay to make an appearance in corsets – so I gently talked him into the car and ran him along to the local police station to see if he was a reported stray. If ever you come across a stray, this is the obvious thing to do. The dog might be a dearly-loved pet and his absence could be causing someone a great deal of anxiety.

As it happened, I needn't have worried. The station sergeant said that Paddy had been seen several times and was quite obviously living rough. He was not officially listed as missing. I told him that I was a vet and would take him home to treat him. The sergeant said splendid, and took my phone number just in case.

On the way back to Denes Close, it became quite obvious that Paddy had been very badly treated, quite apart from his wounds, which turned out to have been inflicted by a shotgun blast at fairly long range. He was suffering from malnutrition, and it took me the rest of the journey to gentle him into realising that I meant him no harm. It always grieves me to see a dog in a state of pain and fear.

When I got home, my first job was to clean him and the wound, which was several days' old and suppurating. Half an hour's careful work extracted eighteen pellets of shot, some of which had penetrated quite deeply. I did not speculate on why someone had tried to kill him, although I had a sneaking suspicion that Paddy might have been worrying sheep.

I put him on a careful diet, with lots of natural diet supplements to build up his depleted reserves of minerals, vitamin and protein. Within a week he looked like a different dog, and I freed him from my intensive care unit and introduced him to the rest of the menagerie. This turned out to be a mistake of some magnitude.

I insist on a certain standard of discipline for dogs – without it they are a menace to themselves and to their owners. If they are part of a community, or a family, they can easily be trained to conform to certain standards. Paddy, however, was very set in his intemperate ways and turned out to be a one-dog pack, and a very considerable handful. Paddy was as mischievous as a cartload of monkeys. He was a tremendous extrovert with a glint of pure intelligence in his eye, but he was also a brawler and an indiscriminate lecher. In the house I could just control him – out of it he acted with all the unrestrained villainy of a Barbary Coast pirate. And he was, like Carlo the cat, also an escapologist with more talent than Houdini.

I was once exercising a beautiful standard poodle bitch called Mimi, from whom I had high hopes of eventually producing a champion. Mimi was in season, and I had her off the lead in a huge field. We were three miles from Denes Close and there were no other dogs around. So all was safe. That's what I thought, anyway. I suddenly saw Mimi, who had been, as usual, as good as gold, lift up her beautiful, aristocratic head and then head for the horizon. Streaking towards her on a joyful collision course was none other than the dreaded Paddy...

I could have stopped Mimi whelping, of course, but it is not my style to interfere with a natural function if I can at all avoid it. So Mimi had her pups, five of them in all, and every single one a big-boned, healthy little pup and limbs of Satan without a doubt. But talk about a mixture! People would look at them in awe. 'Yes, they are lovely,' they would say, 'but what on earth are they?' I used to answer, in pretended astonishment at their ignorance, 'Why, can't you see – they're Paddy's.' But, for all that, it stretched my ingenuity and powers of persuasion to the utmost to find good homes for the fruits of that unfortunate and ultra-democratic liaison.

Paddy was like a very few men. He was one of the small breed of rugged individualists who would bend any system to suit themselves. If he had been a man, he would have made a superb partisan, but within the structure of any disciplined army he would probably have been court-martialled and shot. One could admire and even love him, but he was very hard to live with. I was constantly amazed at the damage that dog could do. One of his favourite tricks was to leap up and nip wasps in half in mid-air. He did this with amazing dexterity, often throwing himself feet in the air to catch them.

I intensified my efforts to find him a good home when one of his wasp-hunting leaps carried him through a window in the large greenhouse. But although Paddy was unique (in my experience anyway), there was a lesson to be learned. I suspected he was a sheep-worrier, so he was unsuitable on a farm. And the thought of him in a town flat was ludicrous. Frankly, I wasn't Paddy's type of owner, either. Fond of him though I was, I just did not have the time to start him on a proper course of training, not with all the other animals to look after and a large veterinary practice to run.

I finally gave Paddy away to a good friend of mine who is a forestry official in Wales. It was definitely Paddy's kind of territory and he led a wonderful life, entirely free from the constraints of morals and civilised behaviour.

Before you seek advice on what sort of dog to get, it would be better first to search your conscience and establish whether you should own a dog at all. It is a sad fact that thousands of perfectly nice, respectable, law-abiding citizens – people who may even be prepared to take out a dog licence – should not own a dog in the first place. First of all : have you really got the time to own a dog? Many people haven't. And I would guess that a high proportion of all new dog owners have no idea of the amount of time they are going to have to devote to their new pet. A dog needs companionship. You can't just leave him alone all day while you go off to work, and then leave him alone again in the evening while you go to the pictures. A lonely dog pines and becomes neurotic – that is an established fact, not just a personal opinion. Remember that a dog needs exercise – at least two good walks a day, and preferably runs. You will have to make sacrifices and be prepared to take him for a walk, even in bad weather or when you just feel like a quiet evening in front of the television. And you will have to train him, too. An undisciplined dog running wild in a city park is a menace to himself and everyone else. But it is not his fault if he does – it's yours for not training him properly. This training takes time and patience, commodities not possessed by everyone.

It is madness to keep an alsatian or dobermann in a tiny city flat or bedsitter, but you would be surprised at the number of times this happens. Smaller dogs, of course, need much less room, but even they must have some space to roam around and a garden is very important.

Some people keep pets for all the wrong reasons. I have often found small, insignificant people who own very large dogs, usually called Killer, Satan, Wolf or something else with connotations of ferocity. In some way the size of their dog and the way they control it boosts their egos.

I used to watch one appalling little man in a homburg hat from the window of The Penthouse. He would regularly walk four of the largest alsatians I have ever seen on the lawns, with them all on a leash in one hand. In the other he carried a leather whip. The dogs looked all the larger compared with their diminutive owner. He used to bully the dogs unmercifully, shouting loud and unnecessary commands. He made them walk along the top of a wall, cracking his whip over their backs like a circus trainer. It was a pantomime, and would have been vastly amusing but for the very real element of maltreatment.

One day the inevitable happened. One of the dogs went for another and all four were swiftly involved in one of the nastiest dog-fights I have ever seen. It was absolute chaos, with people scampering clear and children crying and that ludicrous little man leaping round shrieking at the animals. Two policemen arrived and the dogs were finally brought under control.

Should that man have been allowed to own a dog? I think not, although the root of the problem is who could stop him? Similarly, I have known women to keep a type of dog simply because it is fashionable; some people even buy coats and dresses to match. These owners have usually no idea at all of how to keep a dog, and it sickens me to see what is probably a courageous little animal being pampered into an early death. If you haven't a garden, don't just always walk your dog around on the end of a lead. Take him into the countryside regularly and let him have a good run with lots of fresh air. This will do you a lot of good, too.

One sometimes reads of dogs who save their masters' lives. I am sure this happens much more than we realise. A properly exercised dog can be as beneficial to its owner as a regular game of golf. The exercise and fresh air help to fight tension and obesity and many other killing ailments.

Please remember that it is an unpardonable lapse to die before your dog. You have a definite obligation to keep fit and not inconvenience him in this way. But if you are determined to go first, make sure you make provision for him for the rest of his life.

Can you afford a dog? They cost more to keep than many people realise. And if you feed him properly as nature intended, and not just on mushy table-scraps and tins of processed meats, it can be quite an expensive routine.

Many thousands of people economise by not buying a dog licence, and the law in this respect is largely unenforceable. The police just haven't the time or the inclination to check on dogs owned without benefit of clergy, as it were. But I think some system should be evolved which makes people buy licences. And they ought to be made considerably more expensive – with the obvious exceptions of old age pensioners and guard- and guide-dogs. If people had to pay for the privilege of owning a dog, it would greatly help to restrict ownership to those who really wanted one. I feel very strongly about this. A law that is largely ignored is a bad law – and bad for dogs, too.

All dogs need fresh meat daily – preferably raw meat at that. They need things like wholemeal cereals and additives to supplement their intake of the essential minerals, vitamins and proteins. Look at it this way. In their natural state, before they were domesticated and fed on the same sort of processed pap which helps to kill us off before our time, dogs lived off natural foods. They caught it themselves. Smaller animals provided the meat, and they ripped chunks off with their powerful jaws and ate them, fur and bones and all. And they were instinctive naturopaths. When they felt ill, their instincts led them to herbs and roots and grasses – nature's abundant medicine chest – where they knew they would find the cure to their own sickness. But they don't do very well these days. A dog would wander a long time through Neasden or Hackney looking for wild parsley or garlic or elderberry. And even then, centuries of domestication have blunted the fine edge of instinct. They need help to eat properly.

This is the philosophy behind Denes, a company which makes herbal products for pets. It sprang from close observation of birds and animals when I was confined to bed with polio. I would lie in bed for hours, surrounded by a menagerie of animals, watching and observing wild life in the big garden through the wide-open french windows. I saw pigeons bending the slender branches of elderberry trees, their plump breasts stained with the purple juice. They weren't eating elderberries because they particularly liked them; it gradually dawned on me that there must be another reason for it. There was, of course. They were storing iron to help fight the winter.

And why did Paddy, an Irish terrier, smell so of garlic? He often smelt like a French chef in a Left Bank bistro. He ate the wild garlic because he had worms and there is no finer cure. *He* knew, and gradually I knew too.

Although it was many years before I started processing the goodness out of natural sources so that nature's ancient cures were available for modern pets, this was the start of my real education.

I am sorry if this reads like a commercial; it is not intended to be. I want only to stress that there is far more to feeding your dog than a tin of dog meat and a handful of biscuits a day. And to do it properly costs money.

Another question the prospective dog owner should ask himself is: do you really *like* dogs? You would be surprised how many people buy dogs on a whim and then tire swiftly of them. All vets are continually being asked to destroy healthy, lovable, intelligent animals for no other reason than that their owner has 'gone off' them. I have known people buy Scotties because they are fashionable, and after a year change them for poodles because they are more fashionable, and in another few months change them for beagles because they are the latest 'in' breed. Cruelty to animals is not always a matter of beating or physical mistreatment. It is far more often a case of ignorance, folly or neglect. Please examine your motives carefully before deciding to get a dog.

If you finally decide that happiness is a dog, you must so arrange things as to allow one member of the breed you decide on to choose you.

There are two obvious decisions to be made. First there is the breed. Second there is the delicate matter of sex. Think about the breed for the moment. If you fancy a big dog, as I have already said, make sure he's going to have plenty of room to grow up in. If you have some rugged young children, think twice before you get a delicate little toy dog. Despite the description he is a dog, not a toy, rumbustious children can do him a great deal of harm, even though they don't realise it. Then there is the question of noise. Some breeds are more vociferous than others, and although all dogs can be trained to be quiet most of the time, you just cannot completely silence a corgi or a lively terrier. If you have tetchy neighbours and a lease that says 'No dogs', ignore both neighbours and lease by all means, but make things easier all round by choosing a quiet breed. Golden retrievers, for instance, or if they are too big, a cocker spaniel, a pug or a whippet. Bazenjis have no bark at all, but personally I think the curious noise they do make is worse than the most frantic yappings of the most excitable terrier.

I had a beagle once that used to bay at the moon. He was a lunatic in the strictest sense of the word. When the moon was bright and full he would sit in a patch of moonlight, throw back his head and howl for hours. No good at all for a block of flats.

If you have neighbours who are addicted to cats, for goodness' sake don't introduce a terrier-cross into the peaceful little community. It will not remain peaceful for long. Some terriers are implacable enemies of cats and, take it from me, though cats often come off best in a battle fought more in play than anger, *no* cat is a match for a determined dog. I have known many dogs which were inveterate cat killers, and of these terriers seemed to predominate.

When it comes to sex – and doesn't it always? – it's a matter of personal preference. Some people say that bitches are more affectionate than dogs, although I have not personally found this to be true. Dogs are certainly less trouble. They do not have to go through the ordeal of being on heat, an awkward time that comes twice a year and lasts three weeks on each occasion. Unless you want to breed, I would advise a dog.

There is another consideration – the amount of grooming that lies ahead. Obviously a wire-haired terrier is going to take up less time than a borzoi, with its beautiful, flowing coat. And you must remember that dogs, like adolescent boys, can't be judged by the length of their hair. In either case, the long-haired variety can turn out to be the biggest handful, and I can assure you that it takes a long-haired dachshund just twenty seconds flat to cover himself with mud on a rainy day. This grooming business is more important than most people think. It has, for instance, led to an almost complete decline in this country of that wonderful breed, the curly-coat retriever. Once, they were a very popular gun dog and a familiar household pet. But their soft, beautifully curly coat would pick up so much mud and vegetation that they went rapidly out of favour and today they are a rare sight. Which is a great pity, because in many respects they were a perfect pet.

I had one once, called Major. He was intelligent and very gentle. He brought me home a baby mole once, and another time a very young kitten. He was so gentle and his mouth so soft that both animals were completely unharmed. We used to say of Major that he was so daft he would show an intruder where the safe was. On one occasion he almost proved the point.

A friend of mine had left behind his briefcase containing some important papers. He came back for them and found the house temporarily empty. But we had left the french windows open. He got in through the windows, found his briefcase, and left me a little note saying what he had done. Major was in the house at the time, he did not know my friend, and I was vastly intrigued to find out his reaction, if any. I rang my friend. 'Tell me,' I said, 'did you see Major?'

'I did indeed,' said my friend, 'a beautiful dog.'

'What did he do when he saw you, a perfect stranger who could have been a burglar?' I asked.

'Well, first of all he brought me an old slipper . . .'

I often thought my friend had been rather foolhardy to ignore all the other dogs who had the run of the house. Some of them would have had him, and no mistake. But he was lucky to encounter only Major, or perhaps my stock of pets, waifs and strays was low at the time.

The numbers of dogs around at Denes Close varied considerably. A busy time was summer, when any RSPCA official will tell you that many callous owners simply desert their pets when they go on holiday, rather than pay boarding-kennel fees. Another busy time is January, when Christmas-present puppies are found not to be such a good idea after all.

When my stocks were running high, I used to consider my

house burglarproof – until some very enterprising gentlemen broke in at night and made off with a moderate haul. The police arrived with dogs and it was a hilarious sight to see the dogs towing their handlers at a brisk gallop on scents which led invariably to the nearest bitch on heat. The police knew when they were beaten and departed sadly after a cup of tea.

We will probably never know the full story, but in due course a scallywag of a mongrel called Patsy presented us with a litter of pups which displayed unmistakable signs of dobermann. The only dobermanns Denes had seen for ages were the police dogs. Ah well, where there's a will there is invariably a way . . .

When you have decided on breed and sex, write to the Kennel Club in London and ask for a list of breeders in your district. Then go along and let some puppies look you over. Let them take your time – it's an important decision for both of you. But a word of warning here. In each litter, four or five lively, eager puppies will stagger forward, wagging their tails, licking your hand and probably leaving little trickles behind them in their eagerness to impress. As you watch they will tussle with each other, roll over, fall about like circus tumblers. But in the far corner one will sit quietly, looking at you appealingly, his head on one side. It is heartbreaking to neglect him, but neglect him you should. For he is the runt of the litter, the weak one. Steel yourself and take one of his strong, healthy brothers or sisters. It will save you much trouble and more heartache in the years ahead.

If you intend to raise a showdog or to breed, you must use every ounce of skill and judgment you possess. There is so much to look for, and with every breed the important points differ. This is an area where even the experts can go wrong, but they will have a better chance of picking a good one than you. So take an expert along – he will enjoy the walk and may charge you a small fee for his trouble. Do listen carefully to what the breeders say. They may seem a formidable bunch of people – women who breed dogs and horses develop a forceful no-nonsense manner that often frightens gentle stockbrokers or timid military men – but they are usually honest, decent, helpful people who will tell you frankly what they think. It is this frankness, of course, which adds to the ferocity of their reputation. But don't be put off by it – they will call a spade a spade, but they won't thump you around the ear with it.

A good friend of mine, though, is undoubtedly a formidable lady. She breeds horses and Afghan hounds and regularly rides with the local hunt. One priceless story is told of her that hardly bears repeating. She returned from the hunt one day and handed her horse over to the groom. It had been a hard hunt and the horse looked very tired. 'The horse looks hot and lathered,' said the groom.

'So would you be, Griffiths, if I'd just ridden you for three hours,' said the lady, and strode off, a bulky and formidable figure in her black habit and hard bowler.

I think I used to be the only person who dared argue with her about hunting. 'Mind your own business, Buster,' she used to say, 'or I'll think twice before I pay your outrageous bill.'

Finally, make up your mind whether you really want to spend money on a pedigree puppy, or whether you would give a good home to some poor old pooch. All animal welfare societies have lists of unwanted dogs, and although they may not win any prizes, they will be as intelligent, faithful and lovable as any champion.

While talking of mongrels, I am always reminded of Percy, a redoubtable dog who may have made British naval history and was surely the only dog to take taxi rides on his own. Percy was owned by a friend of mine who was the captain of a tank landing-craft in Italy during the last year of the war. He was based on the Adriatic and his job was regularly to ferry tanks and other military material across the Adriatic. One day he acquired Percy, or rather Percy acquired him. He simply waddled on board, was made a huge fuss of by the crew and recognised a good berth when he saw one. Thereafter Percy became the ship's dog and contributed to crew morale. He made frequent excursions ashore where, like any self-respecting sailor he probably had an amour in every port. But he seemed to know about sailing schedules and always arrived back in time for the next trip. But one day Percy didn't turn up. The skipper anxiously surveyed the dockside and even delayed sailing for a time, but in the end the ship sailed minus its dog. There was little enemy activity in those waters at that time, but Percy had become a good-luck mascot as well as a pet, so the crew had an anxious voyage. On the way back, they sighted a sister ship which usually occupied the next berth. It was on its way back to England but appeared to be several miles off-course. Anyway, the skipper was just about to flash 'Bon voyage' when the other ship started signalling. And the signal read, 'We've got Percy.' So, in mid-ocean, the two ships came together and Percy was formally transferred to the twitter of a bosun's pipe. The Royal Navy have always done things right. Then, with Percy safely restored to his own ship, they steamed off to get on with the war.

When the war was over, the captain kept the dog. In fact, he added two dachs to his family, but there never was a character like Percy. On one occasion the whole family were settled down in front of the fire about to consume some poached eggs. Percy, who was fat and greedy, demonstrated that he wanted to eat, too. Suddenly, one of the poached eggs shot off a plate and fell squarely on Percy's head. The yolk ran down his ears and Percy was twisting about like a professional contortionist in his efforts to get some. But, to add insult to injury, the dachs pounced and licked it off him. He was much aggrieved and sulked for the rest of the night. Percy, in fact, was accident-prone. When he was in a car he always rode in the back seat, with the other dogs in the front, for Percy was very jealous of his privileges. One day, on their way to the woods for a walk, his mistress was forced to brake hard to avoid a cyclist who swerved across in front of the car. Percy shot forwards from the parcel shelf, inadvertently opened the car door with his body and fell out on to the road. His mistress had started to accelerate after braking but saw Percy roll out in her mirror. She stopped immediately. Percy rolled over and over, picked himself up, had a good shake, watered a tree and calmly jumped back in the car. It was as if the whole incident had been arranged entirely for his benefit.

Percy was no stranger to central London because his mistress always took him on shopping expeditions. He was so well-trained that he walked reliably without a lead. But one day she lost him in Oxford Street. She searched everywhere and picked up a clue in her bank where a cashier who knew her said Percy had popped in, had a good look round and then left. She informed the police and then sadly returned home. She had barely unlocked the door when there was a squeal of brakes outside and a taxi pulled up. And sitting inside was Percy. Apparently he had trotted calmly to a taxi rank which his mistress often used and hopped in the open luggage compartment. The driver recognised him, waited a time and then drove him home. His mistress was overjoyed to get him back but Percy treated the whole thing as a matter of course. It must have been his Royal Navy background.

I have just finished reading a very remarkable book about bull-fighting, a sport which I loathe. It is written by El Cordobes, a man who is a hero in his native Spain and, although the underlying theme is one of cruelty to bulls and horses, it cannot detract from the courage and perseverance of an amazing man. I met him once in Marbella and was prepared to dislike him on sight. However I must admit I liked him. I found him a very complex person. The man who had killed thousands of noble bulls was heartbroken over a missing dog. As it happened, I was able to help him.

It had started five or six days previously. We were staying in a bungalow in the grounds of the Marbella Club and one morning I saw a boxer bitch looking as forlorn as only boxers can. It turned out that she had reason to look upset – she had a broken leash round her neck and was obviously a stray. To complicate matters even further, she was in season, which is the worst possible time for a beautiful bitch to wander. Naturally, we took her home and kept her indoors during her most dangerous period. Meanwhile, I made inquiries round the club but got nowhere. It looked like the old firm was in business again – we seem to attract strays in foreign climes, and there is always the fearful problem of what to do with them when the time comes to go home. One evening, with the boxer secure indoors, we were invited to dinner in the main club. We stopped when greeted by the Duke and Duchess of Windsor who were dining there, and then the club's owner, Prince Alphonso, took us proudly over to meet his national hero, El Cordobes. He was recovering from a bad goring and still looked rather shaky. Despite my opinion of bull-fighting I found him charming. Then he told me the main reason for his depression – his boxer bitch had run away from his home several miles from the club and he had a terrible feeling that he would never set eyes on her again. I was absolutely delighted to inform him otherwise. El Cordobes and his dog had a joyful reunion and he was very grateful indeed. So grateful, in fact, that he offered us a sheaf of tickets for a big bull-fight shortly. He was quite upset when we refused.

When I told friends about this incident afterwards, they seemed to think I'd missed a splendid opportunity to tell him a thing or two about bull-fighting, and how cruel and unnecessary it was. But it was not for me, a guest in a foreign country, to say anything about a national sport. I saw another side of El Cordobes, a man who grieved at a missing dog, and having met him I know his profession was imposing its own penalties in terms of injuries and tension. To tell you the truth, I felt rather sorry for him; he is paying in full the price of his fame.

Spain is not a gentle country, and the Spanish outlook is very different from ours. But as regards blood sports there is less excuse for our national varieties, which are always most unequal combats between men and dogs and wild animals which are denied the dignity of fighting back. One would hardly class a hare or a fox as formidable creatures.

I hate all kinds of blood sports. If people fancy a cross-country gallop on a horse then good luck to them – it can do their livers and the animals nothing but good. But why does the presence of a pack of dogs and a poor little fox generate such enthusiasm? And what civilised man can get any pleasure in dragging a badger from its hide with a huge pair of tongs and then standing by while it is battered to death or ripped to pieces by dogs?

Cock-fighting is another obnoxious 'sport' which goes on in England to this day. The fact that it has long been made illegal seems to me to be completely illogical if fox-hunting and hare-coursing are allowed to continue. It all depends on which sport can produce the most powerful lobby, and as some very important and influential people form the backbone of hunting I can see little prospect of Parliament forbidding it. Cock-fighting, being a minority sport, was made illegal simply because it lacked powerful support and not because most people found it repugnant. The majority of people dislike hunting, but they don't get anywhere. Puerto Rico, incidentally, is a country where cock-fighting still flourishes and I once saw a cock being prepared by having vicious two-inch spurs strapped on its legs. The natives bet heavily on the birds and tourists find no difficulty in attending a cock-fight. I am sure any normal person would find it a degrading spectacle.

So much cruelty to animals is completely unnecessary. Whenever I see a woman in a sealskin coat I think of the seal barks and those big, brown eyes looking up trustingly at the man who is going to batter them to death.

Another thing I strongly dislike are performing animals and people who use them for props. At Las Palmas once there were two seafront photographers who would pose tourists with their tame lion. This poor creature was mangy and emaciated and anything but a king of beasts. It looked to me to be half doped and I always felt sorry for it. One day a friend of mine had to go to the local vet. This man proudly showed her the results of a recent operation – twenty claws, four canine and some molar teeth. Apparently the poor lion had begun to protest against its treatment and had been swiftly divested of its only means of defence. I was profoundly shocked by this: what a truly awful existence for a noble animal.

Luckily, there is another side to the picture: the many, many people who treat pets as they should and who derive great pleasure in return. A man and his pet should be a give-and-take relationship. I really don't want to sound like a wet blanket, but I have seen far too much of the sad results of owning unwanted pets. Remember that lovable little puppies and kittens grow up into dogs and cats, and that it will cost you time and money to look after them properly.

A very good friend of mine who adores dogs is Dora Bryan, the famous actress/comedienne who lives in Brighton. Whenever I am ill and in hospital, I can usually count on a letter from Dora in her large, sprawling handwriting that is guaranteed to cheer me up. I try not to miss Dora's television appearances, but she was once appearing in a panel game on TV which I completely missed. However, she told me all about it in a letter while I was languishing in Midhurst Hospital. The question master asked Dora what was the first thing she did when she woke up in the morning. Dora replied: 'Well, I cuddle Fred.'

The question master was puzzled. 'But I thought your husband's name was Bill,' he said.

'It is,' said Dora. There was an embarrassed silence until Dora added: 'Fred's my schnauzer . . .'

Ask a silly question . . .

Chapter Ten

FETES WORSE THAN DEATH

Judging at properly organised dog shows, of which of course Crufts is the outstanding example, I used to enjoy enormously, but I was often less enamoured with some of the requests to officiate at strange, fête-type functions where it was cucumber sandwiches on the vicarage lawns, heavily spiced with acute boredom.

Nevertheless these rural bunfights were usually in an excellent cause and not without elements of humour. I think the strangest thing I ever saw was a 150-pound pig tearing an enormous path of destruction across the nurtured lawns and flower beds of a big house in the heart of Kent. It all started with a phone call from someone I shall call Lady X. The anonymity is necessary to protect our friendship, because she would certainly never forgive me for taking the lid off her fête and stirring up the dust of many years ago.

Lady X was a great fête thrower. She was president at the very least of a score of local organisations, and for each the crowning glory of the year was a fête in Her Ladyship's grounds. There were so many every summer, it was a bit like the continuing story of Peyton Place.

Anyway, Lady X asked me to come and open the fête, officiate at the dog show and generally make myself useful. She was finding celebrities were getting a little thin on the ground where her fêtes were concerned, which must be why she asked me. But the cause was excellent and Lady X was an old and valued client. So I said yes, without the slightest knowledge of what I was letting myself in for.

I often thought that Her Ladyship had friends in the very highest places and had some sort of reciprocal arrangement with God, because all her fête Saturdays were blessed with perfect weather. And so was this – a perfect day in midsummer when the gardens glowed with colour and the lawns were as green and as flat as billiard tables.

The fête started well enough. She made her set speech and

declared the proceedings well and truly open. I think representatives from every Women's Institute in the county were present, all wearing hats of astonishing design and variety. Then it was my turn. I was just winding up when I saw behind the audience a figure emerge from the french windows of the house. The figure was crawling on all fours clutching a bottle. It was none other than His Lordship. I absolutely didn't know what to do. I had enough sense to realise that if I stopped speaking everyone would turn round to get on with the fête, in which case they couldn't avoid seeing the old chap, who at this stage had reached a flower bed and had either passed out or fallen asleep. So I continued talking desperately, at the same time scribbling a note to Lady X to the effect that her husband had been taken ill on the flower bed outside the study and would she do something to avoid a scandal? Still frantically speaking, and only too aware that the audience were getting restive, I leaned over and passed the message to Lady X. She didn't bat an eyelid. She sort of drifted away without attracting attention, and two minutes later two servants seized His Lordship without ceremony and bundled him into the house. I managed to stretch things out until Lady X slipped demurely back into position, by which time the day was saved but the audience were practically paralysed with boredom.

And just one hour later, His Lordship, who had made a remarkable recovery, walked graciously round the stalls and sideshows as if he had never touched a drop of the hard stuff in his life. He invited me into his study for a drink, and the place was as well stocked as a West End hotel bar, complete with a huge keg of beer on polished mahogany trestles.

I judged the dog show in a big marquee. It was very, very different from Crufts, of course, and the classes included the best-dressed dog, the dog with the waggiest tail and the dog with the most soulful eyes. These proceedings were considerably enlivened when a dreaded Kerry blue, with scar tissue instead of a face, tore loose from its owner and proceeded to attack every other animal within reach. Most of the other dogs were on the leash, and the pandemonium was indescribable. The labrador of one tall, very thin lady took about ten turns of its lead round her legs and she finally toppled to the ground, for all the world like a maypole in distress. I think the dogs thoroughly enjoyed themselves, and one standard poodle with a ruffled jacket and ribbons battled with the Kerry blue with great courage, reminding me of a French dandy fighting off a villainous great pirate. Things were finally brought under control and the Kerry blue and its embarrassed owner were politely thrown out. And in the best traditions of show business, the show went on.

Actually, it went on and on. Without time for a cup of tea which at this stage I sorely needed, I helped to judge the village beauty queen competition, which went on amid roars and cheers from the local youths, all of whom had clearly been imbibing deeply at lunchtime. It was one of these, I suspect, who introduced the final factor which set the seal of success or failure on the fête. Which it was I personally am undecided, and will leave the final judgment to you.

Traditionally, a bowling-alley had been set up, and the idea was to bowl hard wooden balls through holes, each of which carried a certain value. The balls cost so much each, and the person with the highest score of the afternoon won a prize. In this case a piglet.

I have always hated this bowling-for-a-pig idea, although I realise it is part of our rural English heritage. I always worry about what happens to the poor little thing afterwards and whether it goes to meet its myriad porcine ancestors without needless suffering from inexpert hands. The pig that was earmarked for first prize was a baby one, and was safe in a pen in a trailer on the back of a Land-rover which had been parked near by. But some comedian introduced an enormous pig into the proceedings. You understand that I did not condone the action. Pigs are animals like any other and I deplore anything that smacks of cruelty. But I would not be human if I did not state that what followed was the funniest thing I have ever seen in my life.

The pig ploughed through the proceedings like a supercharged tractor. People scattered like confetti in a stiff breeze as the berserk animal cut great swathes of destruction across lawns and flower beds. Everything that stood more than four feet off the ground was clustered with people, just like life rafts after a shipwreck. The Land-rover with the baby pig in the back groaned visibly under its burden. Lady X stood on the roof of a parked car, bellowing instructions to her staff and they scuttled round trying to corner the pig. It finally cornered itself by bursting into the flower-show tent and bringing the whole construction down on itself. Even then it took half a dozen stalwart retainers to lead it to safety.

Many thought it indeed a superb fête; quite Lady X's best effort. Before I left I peeped into the study. His Lordship was fast asleep in a huge leather armchair, a beatific expression on his face, and a quart pewter tankard nestled in his lap like a baby. On the way back I was struck by a sudden, dreadful suspicion. Could it have been His Lordship who engineered the . . .? But no, surely not.

Dog shows are part of the English country scene, but it would be very wrong to confuse the novelty shows with the real thing. There is a lot of prestige and money attached to successful breeding and exhibiting, and where money creeps in, then it is often followed by villainy. Some breeders are up to every trick in the book, and all judges have to keep their wits about them in order that justice is seen to be done.

I was about to go on one of my periodic visits to Paris when a Californian breeder contacted me. He said he was thinking of buying a certain poodle from an English breeder in France and asked me my opinion of it. To be absolutely on the safe side, I made an appointment with the breeder and looked it over. The price was high. Prices usually are for the American market on everything from vintage cars to souvenirs of Stratford-on-Avon. However, the dog looked very good to me in every way and I really couldn't fault it. I wrote to the Californian breeder to that effect and he bought the dog on my recommendation. I did not accept a fee and treated it simply as a favour. It is not a simple thing to ship a dog from France to California, and there are many shipping formalities and health regulations to be met. So it took quite a time before the breeder was able personally to look over his investment. And he didn't much like what he saw. By the time he got the dog, its black coat had started turning grey. The journey hadn't taken *that* long.

It turned out that the dog's back and leathers (ears) were turning grey prematurely, and a closer look revealed traces of black dye. Either the previous owner had cunningly concealed a natural defect and won many honours with the dog on completely false pretences, getting a selling price quite out of proportion to the dog's true worth, or, as I suspect, he had substituted another dog which I had examined.

This episode taught me a lesson – that not all breeders are honest and one must keep very wide awake when judging. In later years I earned the reputation of being a tough judge, and much preferred this to being called lax. But there are always people who will try to beat the rules, and I often wonder just how many people have used undiscovered devices to conceal a flaw which would have stopped an otherwise perfect dog from winning a championship.

I was rather green in my early days as a judge, and when you come to think about it the judicious use of dye is an obvious ploy. But one trick which is virtually undetectable is tattooing. I heard about a London tattooist who made a lot of money tattooing sailors and drunks by night, and dogs, in conditions of great secrecy, by day. Many owners found that a tattoo was very useful, particularly with boxers, because a tiny white mark would ruin a dog's chances.

I discovered this purely by accident when I was practising. About four people asked me to prescribe dope for their dog within a relatively brief period, and eventually I became curious. I asked why. Two people told me quite frankly that they were going to have their dog's noses tattooed, and that the artist asked them to bring along an anaesthetic to keep the dog quiet during the brief but painful operation. I was quite horrified, particularly as this trick appeared to be so widespread. I expect it still goes on. I for one know of no way of detecting a tattooed nose in the show ring.

One lady who had clearly never heard of tattooing but was nevertheless very inventive presented me with a beautiful dachshund for judging. I opened the dog's mouth to look at its teeth and the back of my hand brushed its nose. It came away covered in soot. Apparently the owner, just before judging, had stuck her finger up a car's exhaust-pipe and rubbed the oily carbon on the dog's nose to cunningly conceal a blemish. I was delighted to have nipped that little dodge in the bud.

One of the cruellest tactics, which I have come across several times, is for a breeder deliberately to tread on a rival dog's foot, so that it will be lame when it enters the ring. I have also heard of someone bribing a kennel maid to doctor a dog's food so that it will be ill and jaded on show day. And once I was offered a considerable bribe. I reported this to the Kennel Club, who took drastic disciplinary action. On a lower key, it is positively amazing how many dinner invitations one gets as a judge when the day of a big show draws nearer. As I said before, villainy follows money as closely as a shadow.

My most curious judging appearance took place at a big dog show at Ballsbridge, Dublin on St Patrick's Day. The Irish craftily guaranteed a record attendance by granting the show a drinks licence in the afternoon, making it the only place in Dublin where one could drink on St Patrick's Day, as opposed to the night.

The episode started on a strange note the previous day when I flew into Dublin as arranged by the organisers. In those days, one needed a passport to enter the Republican part of the Emerald Isle and I unfortunately had forgotten mine. There are two disparate groups of Irishmen – the vast majority, who not only do not give a bejabers for red tape but actually mutilate it, and a small section of officialdom which actually reddens it. I had the misfortune to tangle with the latter. I was practically arrested and almost deported whence I had so lately come. It took me ages to establish my bona fides, assisted by fellow judges who responded to my frantic telephone calls and dashed over to vouch for me in person. The customs men finally and with great reluctance let me enter, but before they did so they confiscated a perfectly harmless book on the Prince Regent's Brighton days. I will never know why, but for some strange reason this book was on the banned list although politics were hardly mentioned and sex less so. Perhaps they are sensitive about Mrs Fitzherbert despite the passage of nigh on a couple of centuries.

However, one thing which is positively unbanned in Ireland is drinking, and the dog show was launched by an official banquet the night before in which drink flowed like the waters of the nearby Liffey. Before every official and judge stood a bottle of John Jamieson whiskey and one was expected to down it like a gentle Chablis. I have never been averse to a drink, although now it's out for me, but I absolutely loathe Irish whiskey. I solved the problem and saved the reputation of the effete British by disposing of some of my ration to a waiter. Indeed, all the waiters were at it and appeared to be outdrinking the guests to establish firm, democratic – republican principles.

The Irish are ever a nation to hold the hour and grab another. So after the banquet and the speeches, the tables were cleared for action and some really serious drinking commenced. After a while I was invited to join a party for a visit to a castle just outside Dublin, and if that structure had possessed a moat then it would have been filled with Guinness. I could not decide whether the fortifications were to stop people getting in, or to stop people getting out. We really had a whale of a time and even I, a champion talker, felt like an amateur in the midst of these convivial, professional conversationalists.

I cannot remember the weather when St Patrick's Day finally dawned, although it was probably raining. But I do remember that practically all the revellers wore dark glasses to insulate their battered senses from the light of day. The dog show itself was absolute chaos. I actually saw a man singeing the coat of his wire-haired dachshund with a huge taper, the stiffness of the coat being an important factor in judging this particular breed. I was particularly amused by his complete lack of precautions. He just stood there singeing away with no one taking a blind bit of notice. It was all very, very different from Crufts.

During the afternoon, it appeared that at least half of drinking Dublin was in attendance, and all in assiduous training for the night's festivities. And came the evening . . . It was a municipal binge of Homeric proportions. Let it never be said that the Irish don't know how to enjoy themselves. They are also hospitable to a fault and I thoroughly enjoyed myself. These days, I am quite sure I haven't another Dublin dog show left in me.

It is a proud boast of mine that I have never been bitten by a dog, despite the grim predictions of some breeders when one wants to inspect their animal's teeth in the show ring. This is a whiskery ploy; they try to stop the judge inspecting a dog's teeth – a most important part of judging – by pointing out that the animal, while perfect in all other respects, becomes as savage as a rabid wolf only when a judge wants to inspect his teeth. I don't know if this trick actually works these days, but it never did with me. A judge has the right to insist on a dental inspection and, of course, most animals don't mind a bit. It's just the owners. If a dog is genuinely a little snappy, the drill is to ask its owner to show the teeth, making sure he does so properly without hiding any flaws.

One of my most awkward jobs came when I was asked to stand in at short notice to judge. I was a little worried because I didn't know what breed I was to judge. This is most important. Although one may know dogs generally and by using a little common sense be very adaptable, it is a fact that, because there are certain points to watch for in certain breeds, judges tend to specialise. I was always well up on dachshunds. My fears crystallised when I turned up and was asked to judge

Australian terriers. I knew very little about this breed, my only practical experience being one owned by Denise Robins and a pair I had treated for an old lady at Feltham. I tried to cloak my ignorance with a fine display of confidence, but I was far from happy. It was all very difficult. I found the dogs slightly snappy and their owners equally formidable. Have you ever noticed how some people, after a long association with a particular breed, begin to take on some of the characteristics? Anyway, I was quite sure an Australian terrier was going to nip me that day and break my record, but I got through unscathed and breathed a deep sigh of relief when it was all over. In fact, I subsequently came to like Australian terriers and several times was asked to judge them again.

In my judging days, I sometimes had for a colleague the famous *Daily Express* pet columnist, Stanley Dangerfield. We used to get on very well together, and I particularly liked his no-nonsense approach. He talks, in fact, just like he writes. Recently he wrote a story in the *Express* about alsatians, at a time when the press was full of atrocity stories about this breed after two guard-dogs had savaged a child. His article was like a breath of fresh air. He pointed out that alsatians are not basically savage, but are large, powerful dogs which require proper handling. They are probably the least suitable dog to be kept in a flat or a small house in a town or city, and any faults could usually be traced to their owners. When I read it I could just picture him delivering this as a verbal blast, and I couldn't have agreed more. Alsatians are superb dogs, but they have to be raised sensibly. And that is the crux of the matter.

I have made many references to Crufts in this book, usually as a standard of comparison. Crufts is far away the greatest dog show on earth and I count myself honoured to have judged there. There is that undefinable air of class about the place which commands respect, and even the dogs are on their best behaviour. Which makes a change, because dogs can be very like children. Despite the best of upbringing, they are always liable to commit a grave social lapse which can be hideously embarrassing to people, although the dogs don't seem to bother.

The biggest lapse I ever saw a dog commit was live on television before a considerable audience. The background to the offence was that I had been judging a show, and afterwards was explaining on television the winning points of the dogs, using the actual animals. It is frowned upon in the show business to enter a bitch on heat, but sometimes it does happen. And when it does, the general effect is to put all the dogs on their worst behaviour; they become very natural indeed. And this is what happened on television. The bitch in question had been all right in the show, but suddenly became less than all right in the TV studio. The effect on a certain dog was immediate. It dashed over full of evil intent and proceeded to initiate a very spirited consummation in front of about ten per cent of the whole country. It was all a bit too dramatic for the programme, which terminated suddenly.

I do hope I haven't painted too grim a picture of breeders as a profession. There are some nasty, unscrupulous ones, as there are in any walk of life, but most of them are perfectly ordinary, decent people. It's just that the ones that aren't make such a profound impression.

It is important to realise just what a critical world the show breeder lives in. Not even Miss World's vital statistics are as vital as those of a show dog. A fraction of an inch more or less in the head, tail, ears or shoulders can make the difference between a champion and an also-ran. A tiny blemish that under normal circumstances would hardly be noticed can make the difference between success or failure. And that, in turn, can have tremendous financial implications. A champion dog is worth hundreds of guineas, whereas a blemished dog is worth very little. This tense world is an understandable reason for some breeders having a pernickety reputation.

They are also a tough lot. I was judging a small show in a dreadful storm with thunder and lightning like the wrath of God. The marquee was leaking like mad and being buffeted by a gale, when the main support pole was hit by lightning. It made a noise like the crack of doom, but the breeders never budged. The show must go on, come hell, hail or high water.

I think my most unpleasant show was at Harrogate. I always tried to avoid the breeders, most of whom I knew very well, before the show. Part of the reason was that it wouldn't do to be seen talking and laughing with one particular breeder in case the others shrieked 'favouritism'. Another part was that I was usually a little tense before a show and just didn't enjoy meeting people in my usual extrovert fashion.

Don't ask me why, but I am addicted to mustard pickles. Like most addicts I try to kick the habit and go without them for months. At other times I will have an insatiable urge and nothing else will do but to buy a jar and start eating. I am particularly fond of the peppery, violent yellow variety. Very bad for one, I'm sure!

Just before the show, I badly needed a mustard pickle fix. So I stopped at a shop and I bought a jar, eating them under somewhat informal circumstances. Needless to say, I spilled canary-yellow mustard pickle all down my jacket. I wore it on my lapels like the Légion d'Honneur. And I was wondering how I could erase the shameful stains when I bumped into a large posse of breeders. It was most embarrassing. But even worse was to come. I was invited to visit the Harrogate Spa, and given a glass of the famous waters which I drank dutifully but with no relish at all. This, plus the pickle, gave me a most uncomfortable day.

It was at a charity show at Southsea that I first met that marvellous singer and entertainer, Harry Secombe. He and Stirling Moss were judging the comic classes and I had been called in to judge the serious side. A big attraction at the show was Stirling's first-ever racing car. There was no one more interested in the car than Moss himself. He didn't know it was coming and had lost touch with the vehicle. It must have been a nostalgic reunion. At that time he was probably the best racing driver in the world and chasing the world championship which so often just eluded him.

Secombe, of course, stole the show with his own particular brand of Goonish humour and that incredible voice when he occasionally burst into song. I told him he was good enough for La Scala, and he looked quite sad for a moment. He told me there had been a time when he wanted to be a top operatic singer more than anything else, but he had decided he lacked the dedication and was certainly earning far more money as a comedian. One is tempted to think 'What a pity', but on re-flection he has a far larger audience as a comic and has brought joy and laughter to millions of people.

After the dog show, which was very well organised and of a surprisingly high standard, I was asked to help judge a bouncing baby competition. The award of best of breed went to a cute little black baby which had the most marvellous teeth. I know more about puppies and kittens than babies, but find them all very appealing.

Chapter Eleven

MOVING HOUSE

We lived in The Penthouse, high above Hove seafront, for ten years. We all loved the place, partly for its spaciousness, partly for the tremendous views. But as far as I was concerned there were a couple of snags. This part of the South coast is subject to sudden summer mists called sea frets, which roll in from the sea like a blanket. They are dank and gloomy and play hell with my chest. It was one of the big disadvantages of living so near to the sea. We would be shrouded in swirling mists, while people a few hundred yards inland were baking in the sun.

The second snag was also connected with the climate. In the winter, The Penthouse was buffeted by the prevailing south-westerly winds which often registered gale force. For days I would be unable to get out and it reminded me very much of living on the Wolf Rock lighthouse. The sea would boom sullen and angry on the shingle, the windows would rattle and everything seemed grey and depressing.

So we decided to move. We decided this in the spring, when the promise of good weather should have shaken our resolve. But it had been an awful winter and we made up our minds. The obvious problem was – where? I had a few ideas, and although part of me was dreading the upheaval, I could see in my mind's eye a sheltered garden with flower beds and trees and herb bed – a picture of Denes Close, in fact. So we decided to go round garden-hunting and then to see if the house also suited.

Ron drove me round Hove and Rottingdean one day when I was full up with barium meal and in between four X-rays. Apart from looking at 'For sale' boards, I was glad not to have to go home. I was so hungry after dieting all the previous day to prepare my stomach for the barium meal that the smell of food would have driven me mad. So we covered many miles in between hospital visits, but saw nothing suitable. I began to get depressed, as well as famished.

Towards the end of the day we were touring Hove, and

driving along a road running along one of the boundaries of Hove Park. The funny thing was I had never seen this road before, although I reckoned I knew the town like the back of my hand from my days in practice at Denes Close. Suddenly, I saw a large detached house which almost certainly would have a big garden at the rear. It was for sale. The day brightened up. I took down the estate agent's name and phone number and contacted him the minute we returned home.

The printed details of the house made it sound like an extension of Buckingham Palace, and it certainly seemed ideal. But there was a slight hitch – the house was practically sold. However, we made an appointment to view and went round the following afternoon. The vendors, to put it in proper estate agent's language, told us that a deposit had been paid, but would we like to see round just in case? We did, and as we toured the house I was mentally knocking down walls, installing a lift and making sweeping alterations. The rear garden had tremendous potential and we went back home and waited with our fingers crossed.

Time went by but we didn't look any further. Somehow, I had a feeling that the house was going to be ours, although the weeks passed like months. Then the agent rang and said were we still interested because there was a chance of the initial purchase falling through? Dorothy immediately put down a deposit, and a week later the house was hers.

And then the trouble started. First, there was the surveyor's report, which gloomily indicated the presence of dry-rot and sundry other house-eating creatures. I always consider surveyors to be a profession of Dismal Johnnies and did not allow the report to upset us. Indeed, the house is still standing. The next step was to find a builder and, as everyone who has embarked on a similar search will know, this can be a very depressing business. We found one, who was highly recommended, and told him what we wanted. Principally, we wanted the sitting-room and study turned into one huge room, provision for a lift, and a garden-room built on to the rear wall of the house. He then told us just why it couldn't be done. Everything we suggested was impossible. And merging the two rooms into one was doubly impossible, because the wall which stood between them was a load-bearing wall and half the house would collapse. He wanted the job all right, but he wanted to do it his way and in his own time. We wanted it our way, and time was getting short because we had a removal date fixed at The Penthouse.

While we were waiting to strike some sort of compromise, Dorothy and I heard of an old-established company in Lewes which made reproduction Adam fireplaces using authentic Adam moulds. We measured up and then went and ordered one. This, at least, was something constructive. We were excited about it because we inspected the firm's products and the craftsmanship was of a very high order. It would be just the thing to embellish our huge new sitting-room.

At this juncture, as if predicting the trouble ahead, my chest seized up again and I was forced to enter Midhurst for a decoke. It was absolutely maddening to have to lie there in idleness knowing that our time at The Penthouse was running out and that nothing was being done at the new house. There was not much constructive that I could do – though at times my hospital room looked like an interior decorator's shop, littered with carpet and wallpaper patterns and little drawings of odd corners.

I gradually realised we would never get anywhere with the builder, so I begged a week-end's leave so that I could contact another. I arrived home and joyfully negotiated with an enthusiastic, live-wire of a builder who said yes to everything as firmly as the first had said no. We were all absolutely delighted.

The biggest job by far was converting the two main downstairs rooms into one. He drew up a plan using an overhead girder and two pillars, which would be decorative as well as useful in that they would support the ceiling and replace the function of the wall.

That same mad, hectic week-end we chose the carpets, curtains and wallpapers, and I went back to Midhurst exhausted but much relieved. Two weeks later I was considered well enough to be allowed back home. Ron collected me, and I couldn't wait to see the house. We went round there first, and as we motored up the steep, sweeping drive, I had a sudden premonition of disaster. And as we stopped in front of the house I saw clouds of dust billowing out of every door and window. I didn't dare go in at first, or I would certainly have choked. Workmen were dashing about all over the place looking like survivors of the blitz.

Disaster indeed had struck. The offending wall had been removed, the ceiling made up and the girder and supporting columns had been put into place. Then half the ceiling had fallen in, together with a huge, old-fashioned fireplace from one of the bedrooms.

We had already decided this must go, although I would have preferred a more conventional exit for the monstrosity. Perhaps the first builder had been right after all and the job was impossible. The mess was appalling, and I was only glad that no one had been standing under the ceiling at the time. That fireplace would have dropped upon him as finally as a guillotine blade. However, the builder, his enthusiasm undiminished, was already making plans for a fresh onslaught, so I went on home in better spirits.

Things went well for a time. The ceiling was repaired, the girder was re-installed and the columns braced in position again. Everything seemed to be going ahead according to plan when disaster struck once more. This time the entire twelve-foot chimney breast upstairs, obviously upset by being robbed of the support of the fireplace, plunged through the attic, through the bedroom and on into the living-room. This time the damage was even more extensive. Once again, it was a miracle that no one was killed. At this stage my blood was up. It just can't happen again, I thought, and reconstruction was ordered to commence. But when it did, it was hampered by a spot of industrial trouble.

Running concurrently with this little setback was more trouble – this time involving the wallpapers. It seemed that everything we ordered, first choice and second, was out of print. Naturally, it took considerable time for the retailer to discover this. It was a maddening situation because the papers were chosen with things like carpets and furniture in mind and to change one usually meant changing the others. This in turn caused more trouble with the carpets. It took ages of worry and frustration to sort it all out.

When we obtained the right wallpaper for the living-room, which was still standing in the most encouraging fashion, the builder said that one of his men was, without doubt, the finest paper hanger this side of the Chilterns. He might just as well have said this side of the Carpathians, because the maestro of the paste pot turned out to be a Rumanian giant who was six feet four tall, about as wide again, and spoke not a word of English. Goodness only knows where the builder found him, and I don't know what he was used to hanging in Rumania. It might have been people, but he certainly couldn't hang wallpaper. He papered the huge room with the most expensive material and was just finishing, obviously proud of his work, when I saw that the pattern did not match up. It wasn't a near miss either; it was yards out. When I pointed this out to him, using sign language and shouting, his face darkened ominously, like a storm over Bucharest. I thought he was going to slosh me with the paste pot. The whole room had to be stripped and redone, and, moreover, it was all done at our expense.

While the battles raged, the new Adam fireplace arrived. It was absolutely exquisite but there was one slight snag. When it was put in position it looked like something out of a doll's house. This, of course, was all my fault. When I measured up I had not taken into account that the room would be twice as large, so the proportions were ludicrously wrong.

However, we got out of this one quite nicely. It fitted perfectly into the dining-room where it has since been much admired. We solved the living-room problem by buying for £15 a handsome old cast-iron fireplace over 100 years old which could have been designed for the job. At £15 it started off being a bargain. Then the builder insisted on removing from it five coats of paint and then applying another five. One week later it looked just like it had before, and when finally installed with marble surrounds, the bargain cost something more than £100.

The catalogue of trouble continued. It was a good thing we didn't believe in omens or we would have been looking for another house almost before the ink on the deeds was dry. Our builder hired on our behalf a huge steel skip, of the type which needs a special lorry to move it. This skip was left outside the front of the house and was paid for by the day. For day after day it seemed to be getting fuller and fuller without the builders contributing much in the way of débris. One day I was looking out of the window and saw a little van scoot up the front drive. It stopped outside the skip and a little man leaped out, opened the rear doors and furtively dumped about half a ton of rubbish into our skip. Then he climbed back in and drove off. I was still pondering on this when it appeared again, and repeated the whole exercise. Obviously the wretched little man was using our skip to dump his rubbish. I banged on the window and shouted, and Ron gave chase unsuccessfully. But it solved the problem of the skip – all and sundry must have been using it while we were paying for it.

Meanwhile, time was running out with great rapidity. I had another fight on my hands with the lift manufacturer, whose specifications for installing the lift involved modifications a lot more drastic than I was prepared for. It really was trouble all the way. Finally, we had to move in before the house was finished – the very thing we had been trying desperately to avoid for months. The lift was not in, my bedroom had wires hanging from the walls, and the garden-room was barely half ready. Actually, everyone else moved in, but not I. I stayed with a friend for two months until all the work was completed.

The next task to be faced was moving all the furniture. Ron, who had joined me as my nurse two years earlier (though I had known him for thirteen years), volunteered to do it for us in what he called 'easy stages'. Stages there certainly were, but none of them was easy. The furniture had to come six floors down from The Penthouse, and some of it was too big to go in the lift. So he staggered down innumerable steps and loaded it into a Bedford van, which was always laden way beyond the Plimsoll Line. If it had been a ship it would have foundered. The van used to chug along the sea front, climb the hill and finally wheeze to the top of the drive on its very last gasp. It took him two weeks to complete the move, and as an epic of endurance it deserved to be ranked with the Seven Labours of Hercules.

Even so, there were distractions. On one occasion, Ron was staggering down the stairs clutching a huge oak chest, which has been in my family for 150 years, when he saw through a window a woman floating fully-dressed and head down about fifty yards out to sea. He dropped the chest and ran like a hare to the beach, diving in with all his clothes on and pulling the woman back to shore. I was watching this drama from my bedroom and hurriedly phoned the police and an ambulance. Before help arrived, he had given the woman artificial respiration and saved her life. Her first words to him were, 'Why did you save me, why did you save me?' Apparently the poor woman was trying to kill herself.

Actually, this was one of the reasons why I wasn't sorry to leave The Penthouse. It gave a magnificent view of the sea to the south and a busy main road to the north, and frequently one saw from the lofty eminence things one would have preferred not to. I watched horrified once while two children who were playing on a particularly dangerous groyne were swept off and out to sea by a big wave. I gave the alarm, but the bodies were never found. On another occasion we saw a speedboat hit a swimmer and the propellor practically take the man's leg off. It was later amputated from the hip. We saw road accidents in plenty and had a grandstand view of the fire which burned the Bedford Hotel to the ground. I wish I had a pound for every statement I gave to the police.

The one big drawback to Ron's removal efforts was there was nowhere to put half the furniture when it arrived at Denesland. Either the paint was wet or the carpets hadn't arrived or the builders were still doing the finishing touches. It was absolute chaos.

With the rest of the family establishing the new house – Dorothy, the cook, the houseman and Hal Higgs, a very dear friend of ours who has since died – Ron and I prepared for a grand auction sale to clear up the remainder of the unwanted furniture, which included some quite valuable antiques. I advertised the sale in the newspaper, and on the day we were busy from morning until night, although it seemed that half the visitors were merely curious and wanted to take a look round. Still, we sold everything, and gave away dozens of pot plants and scatter cushions and lampshades to people who made a major purchase. Towards the end of the day, a group of hippies strolled in and bought some stuff, offering cheques in return. I was a little worried about this, but didn't like to insist on cash. As it happened, not one of the cheques bounced, although I cannot say the same for a couple which were tendered by people who looked eminently respectable. It just goes to show.

Right in the middle of the sale, when things were at their most hectic, I had a phone call from Dame Gladys Cooper. We had never met before, although we had dozens of mutual friends, and Dame Gladys asked if she could come and see me because she liked my book and had only just heard where I lived. I told her we were in the middle of chaos, but she wouldn't take no for an answer. I would have much preferred to entertain her in a more suitable setting, but there was little I could do about it without being discourteous. So Dame Gladys arrived with Elizabeth Allan, who of course was no stranger to The Penthouse, although she had never seen it before in such a shattered condition and almost totally denuded of furniture. But I need not have worried about meeting Dame Gladys under such conditions. We got on splendidly, and she told me all about the animals she had owned – almost as many as I had! She wrote to me later, thanking me for taking the trouble to see her, and included two photographs taken of her in Africa. She was posing with Julie, the chimpanzee star of the film *Daktari*, and they were exchanging shell necklaces.

The day after the sale was dealers' day. I had made appointments with two antique dealers and kept back the items I thought were more valuable than the rest, although several times I had been offered good money for them from the general public at the sale. However, I was right out of luck. One dealer forgot the appointment; the other turned up at the wrong address – he went to see a vet with a name similar to mine miles away. I couldn't contact them because it was Saturday morning – their shops were closed and I didn't know their home addresses. We had to be out of The Penthouse by ten o'clock on the Monday morning, so I finally sold the lot at a ridiculous price to another dealer that afternoon. I could have kicked myself afterwards; I'm afraid I will never make a good businessman.

Anyway, we made the deadline and handed over the keys with time to spare. It was the end of The Penthouse and the beginning of Denesland. It had nearly been the end of me, too. It took me a long time to get over the move and I have vowed never again to repeat it. In the end, though, it was worth all the trouble because we have all been very happy at the new house. But the gremlins hadn't finished yet . . .

Hoover and the rest of the tropical fish were moved in their tank, which was installed in a specially prepared recess in one wall of the new garden room. Everything was switched on, the oxygen started bubbling merrily and the temperature quickly climbed to 85°F. Then the tank suddenly collapsed, dumping gallons of water and several dozen astonished fish on to the brand new carpet. Clearly the situation called for swift emergency measures. All hands went to work, scooping up fish and plonking them into warm water in the sink. Ron dashed off to get another tank of the same dimensions, and eventually the fish were replaced and the tank re-installed with no more trouble. Every single fish survived the happening, which speaks volumes for their constitutions. The only casualty was the nice new carpet which, from that day on, has always carried the suspicion of a stain.

My animals made the move with less drama, although I have already explained how Puddy went right off me the moment we left his beloved seafront, and has never forgiven me. He used to be the epitome of the one-man dog. I find it very sad, and know for an absolute fact that Puddy would swop the whole of the Denesland garden for that small section of shingle-studded promenade . . .

Polly, however, was delighted. He never liked the sea breezes which used to ruffle his feathers and he positively loathed the strident seagulls. He took to the sheltered garden like a duck to water, and now chats to the other birds in raucous English. He is particularly friendly with the collared doves which regularly feed on the crumbs at the bottom of his perch. Sometimes Polly lays on a demonstration of static aerobatics, looping the loop on his perch and then regarding the cheeky sparrows with his head on one side as though thinking, 'I know you can fly, but can you do that?'

I don't know if emotions chase ponderously through the horny heads of tortoises, but I am sure that Bert and Eli were also pleased with the move. Bert was a well-travelled tortoise – I brought him back from South Africa – and perhaps the wide open spaces of the garden reminded him of home, because he embarked on some epic overland treks accompanied faithfully by Eli, who was a bit of a provincial, originating in a Hove pet shop. They eventually settled down in the kitchen garden and played havoc with the greens.

The kitchen garden was very much a going concern before we moved in, because as soon as we bought the house we contacted Tom, our engine-driver gardener from Denes Close days, and he was delighted to rejoin us after a ten-year lapse. While we were in the agonies of the move, Tom was placidly turning the kitchen garden into a most productive plot, which enabled us to eat fresh vegetables right from our first meal.

Well, nearly. In fact, the vegetables were simmering quietly along with the rest of our first evening meal on the cooker, when the huge, heavy hood designed to extract 'Cooking smells at source' fell off the wall and demolished the dinner. It also nearly demolished the cook, who had to be revived with copious draughts of that traditional British stimulant, French brandy.

However, it was lovely to be in at last. The very same day that I moved in, with the lift installed and everything working beautifully, Olive Gilbert, the famous contralto, came round and presented us with some lilac trees and a gorgeous magnolia. These were immediately planted in the front garden.

They didn't stay there long, however. That night we were just about to go to bed, when I heard a very familiar noise. It was a cow mooing. I said to Dorothy: 'I know it's very peaceful here compared with The Penthouse, but a cow is ridiculous!' We investigated, and found a very lively heifer which had eaten the magnolia and was munching its way through the lilac. We phoned the police – it was just like old times – and they didn't even bat an eyelid when we told them we had found a heifer in the middle of Hove. They arrived in strength, and cups of tea were made. Meanwhile, Ron had lassooed it to stop the creature wandering further, and at first it was just like a rodeo with the heifer bucking and kicking and Ron being jerked this way and that like a cowboy at branding time. The police contacted the farmer by the simple expedient of ringing the nearest farm – elementary, my dear Watson – and he arrived with a tractor and barred trailer to restore it to its friends. The episode lasted three hours, and must have made an indelible impression on the neighbours.

Shortly after this incident, I was feeling most upset by Puddy's behaviour and made up my mind to get another dog. I heard of a golden retriever in kennels in Staffordshire which had been owned by a couple who had split up and divorced. The dog needed a good home and, as I love this breed, I

arranged to have him on approval. There was a time when I wouldn't have been so cautious, but I felt I wasn't active enough to start training a big dog from scratch.

The dog turned up, and he was certainly a magnificent animal. The first thing he did, when introduced to the garden, was to dig up a major earthworks on the lawn. That was how he got his name, Digger Dene. Thus christened, he proceeded to go from bad to worse. He was a shocker, completely unruly and undisciplined, and toppled me out of my wheelchair twice.

I stretched his approval period time and time again without really deciding to keep him. His saving graces were his good nature and the fact that he and Puddy struck up an immediate friendship. Puddy uses him as a pillow on the rare occasions that Digger Dene lies down.

Several times I almost made up my mind to give him to a farmer when, as dogs sometimes will, he suddenly changed. It was a Hyde to Jekyll transformation, too, and he became almost magically gentle and obedient and showed all the other splendid attributes of the breed. It's almost as if the dog knew when he'd gone far enough and decided to turn over a new leaf to avoid any unpleasant consequences. Today, Digger is one of the very best dogs I have owned; and it seems impossible that he was ever wilful or naughty. Puddy still sleeps on him, incidentally.

Our pets were extended by the gift of two bantams, Cocky and Henrietta. They lived in the garden and slept together up a holly tree. They were very tame, lovable birds and every day presented us with one lovely little brown egg, which we took it in turns to eat. I had owned bantams nearly all my life and one can get very fond of them indeed.

One night tragedy struck. We heard a fearful racket, but it wasn't sufficient for me to get out of bed. The dogs started barking, and Ron got up and let them out for a time in case it was an intruder trying to break in. Things quietened down, the dogs came back and we all went back to sleep. But the following morning, Cocky and Henrietta were missing. All we found was a pathetic little pile of feathers at the bottom of their holly tree. It was obvious that a fox had killed the pair of them. There is nothing surprising in foxes marauding into built-up areas. Parts of Brighton and Hove have been plagued with them for years. They slink in looking for domestic scraps of food and probably do better scavenging from dustbins than they do in the country. A couple of little bantams would be easy pickings for any fox.

Now that we have the garden as we want it, one of our greatest pleasures is sitting out looking at the birds. We have counted forty-eight different species, some of them quite rare. We encourage them, of course, by putting out food. Dorothy is officer commanding rations for birds, and buys vast quantities of food.

One of the side results of running a free house for birds is the number of squirrels who pop in for a meal. Sometimes we are positively plagued with them, and the cheeky little things pinch the bird food and eat their heads off. They are nuisances, but they looked so appealing I cannot find it in me to take reprisals.

So the move was all worth while in the end. Despite the inauspicious omens, we have all found much happiness at Denesland, and the garden with its trees and flowers and animals reminds me very much of my beloved Denes Close.

Life here is far more peaceful and serene than at The Penthouse with its grandstand views of storms in the Channel, drownings just off the shore and traffic accidents on the crowded roads.

We have only had the police twice, when the heifer ate the magnolia tree, and for the parrot on the roof.

And we still have a view of the sea through the trees, without having the noise of the seafront traffic or the crashing of rough seas on the shingle at night.

Chapter Twelve

MY BRIGHTON FRIENDS

I know of no finer place in which to live than Brighton and Hove. Although they are two completely separate towns, they both tend to get lumped together as Brighton, much to the chagrin of the Hove Council who are always fighting stubbornly to retain the town's identity. Brighton is gay and lively, fascinating architecturally, and with an ambience all its own. Hove is its quiet sister, and between them the towns boast more celebrities as residents than any other place I can think of. This, of course, is a large part of Brighton's charm. And one of the main reasons for its popularity is its proximity to London. They tell me the late night train from Victoria has a passenger list which reads like a *Who's Who* of the theatre, although I cannot personally vouch for that. It is thirteen years since I last travelled on a train and I would dearly love to repeat the experience.

I wonder if Prinny knew what he was starting when he treated Mrs Fitzherbert to that little place in the country which is called the Royal Pavilion. What a woman she must have been to help inspire that architectural extravaganza which turned a little fishing village into a prince's playground.

I can think of no better way to introduce some of Brighton's many celebrities than to describe the guest list at a party we gave a while ago. Initially, it was going to be a discreet, informal affair, but like all good parties it swiftly developed into something spectacular with enough celebrities to make a dowager gasp.

The first guests to arrive were Jack Hawkins with his wife Doreen, who are frequent week-end visitors to Elizabeth Allan (known to her friends as Liz) and her husband, Bill O'Bryan. I think Jack Hawkins is a tremendous man, and a man of formidable courage. The way he fought against cancer must be an inspiration to thousands of people. Jack lost his wonderful voice when he had cancer of the throat. He was operated on and the cancer removed, but he lost his voice completely.

With enormous courage and faith and hard work, he learned to speak again, projecting the sounds from his diaphragm. His wife fought with him every step of the way. I remember I was at a party with Terence Morgan and Jack's wife shortly after Jack had phoned her from Hollywood and told her his voice was getting worse and he had undergone a series of tests which confirmed in his own mind that he had that unmentionable disease. Doreen, despite this appalling burden, battled bravely on, but it was clear she was under a considerable strain. When Jack went in for his operation, he showed the same courage and fortitude he has so often portrayed on the screen. Liz and Bill went up to see him as soon as was possible, and reported that he was in tremendous spirits. Apparently his first gesture when he regained consciousness indicated a demand for a cigarette and a glass of champagne. What a man!

Another person of considerable courage who embellished the party was Kay Hammond, who had been rather ill for some time, although you would not think so to look at her. She always dresses superbly and looks absolutely radiant. It was a touching sight to see her husband, Sir John Clements, looking after her and seeing she was not getting overtired.

In fact, when people talk about the high marriage casualty rate in the theatre, I always think of people like Jack and Doreen Hawkins, Kay Hammond and John, Bill and Liz O'Bryan, and many, many others. You could go a long way to find more devoted couples. I suppose it's the same as everything else; if people want to make a marriage work they will, even in a profession as demanding as the theatre.

The party was becoming more and more animated when Dame Flora Robson arrived accompanied by her Manchester terrier. Jackie is large for the breed and I have always had niggling doubts about her ancestry, although she has a pedigree as long as your arm. Not that it matters, because Dame Flora adores the dog and they are inseparable companions. She drifted over immediately to chat to Jack Tripp and Alan Christie, who are my favourite comedians. I travel miles to see their shows, knowing that I will laugh my sides sore during the course of the evening. Why they don't top the bill at the London Palladium, I shall never know. The three are good friends although, before they first met, Jack and Alan wondered what on earth they would have in common with Dame Flora. They worried about the depth of the gulf between Flora's tremendous dramatic acting skills and their own brand of popular comedy. But of course there is no gulf at all – they are all gifted performers and among the very best of their profession.

Suddenly, with entirely suitable drama, Marie Lohr made one of her superb entrances. She is a big, handsome woman dressed, on this occasion, in black, with a rich, dark brown voice which has thrilled thousands of theatregoers in the past. It was the sort of entrance which draws all eyes. Marie declined a cigarette with regal grace and delved into an old-fashioned dorothy bag, from which she took an exquisite Georgian silver snuff box and a tiny silver spoon. She measured a spoonful of snuff and sniffed it as elegantly as a Ming Dynasty princess sipping a delicate infusion of jasmine tea from translucent china. Everything Marie does, she does with consummate style. There are no sneezes, no suddenly watering eyes, because Marie is not prey to the discomfitures of mere mortals. She offered me a pinch and I took it, becoming immediately convulsed with a paroxysm of sneezing. Well, some of us have it and some of us don't. Marie has been taking snuff for more than fifty years, and she estimates she has sniffed at least a hundredweight. Her snuff is especially blended for her by the best firm in the business.

There is a curious sideline to her habit. She used to be highly vulnerable to colds and chills – so much so that she worried about her career. But since she started taking snuff, she has never had a cold again. Perhaps this is the cure for the common cold that doctors are ever searching for.

The man holding a glass of dry sherry to the light was Clive Brook, whom one could call the father of the modern cinema. He is an incredible eighty-two and appears to know the secret of eternal youth. His back is as straight as a ramrod and he swims daily and regularly takes long walks. He has a tremendous zest for life and the only evidence of passing years is that he is going a little thin on top. He was with his wife, Milly, who is wearing as well as he is (another show-business marriage which has stood the test of time). He is one of the very few surviving actors who starred in both silent films and those new-fangled 'talkies'.

Another guest who had entertained people for many decades was 'Duggie' Byng, the man who paved the way for the success of Danny La Rue by originating the concept of female impersonation, now commonly known as drag. In Duggie's heyday, the whole thing was very risqué, but those were the days when people could hardly blink without drawing shocked attention. Not that it worried Duggie. He is now in his seventies and still a most amusing character with a fund of stories about the theatre in the twenties and thirties. After a few drinks, Duggie sang his party piece, 'Doris, the Goddess of the Wind', and we all rolled about, as usual.

Michael Denison and Dulcie Grey were there – yet another devoted couple. Just a few days before writing this Michael and Dulcie rang to say that Titus, their beloved labrador, had died peacefully at the ripe old age of sixteen. They were very upset. Titus was wished on them as a puppy, and he grew up to be the most travelled dog in the history of the theatre. They took him everywhere, and when they were appearing together, he always chose to stay with the one whose dressing-room was the more comfortable.

Titus last year horrified my own dogs at Denesland by gobbling a most unnatural diet of home-made cakes. We were all in the garden enjoying the sunshine with a heavily laden tea-trolley standing by in the garden room. Titus, despite being almost blind, sniffed them out and ate a tray-full of cakes – cream puffs, gingerbreads, macaroons, everything you could think of. Digger Dene, my own golden retriever, stood by looking at this gastronomic piracy in absolute astonishment, while Puddy's nose turned up even further in disgust. Titus, apparently, was very partial to a cake and was unlikely to worry about the source.

Brenda de Banzie, another of Brighton's notable residents, was at the party with her husband, Rupert, who is a well-known theatrical agent. Brenda had a pekingese for many years, but she was so upset when the little chap died that she vowed she would never have another. That was a long time ago, but Brenda has stood by her vow. To this day, she cannot bear even to talk about dogs.

Brenda was talking to Bobby Howes, the former musical-comedy star and father of the charming Sally Ann, whom I had last seen when she came to tea after finishing a day's filming in Brighton for *Chitty Chitty Bang Bang*.

Another guest was Dame Anna Neagle and her husband, the impresario and film producer, Herbert Wilcox. They were talking to Evelyn Laye — Boo to her friends — who was making one of her frequent visits to Brighton to appear in a new play at the Theatre Royal, where many of the pre-London shows are staged. What wonderful, glamorous ladies they are! They have graced so many shows and given them charm and dignity whenever they have appeared.

The guest of honour at the party was a famous American film star, who, for reasons which soon become apparent, had better remain anonymous. He was about to star in a notable comedy rôle, although he didn't know it at the time.

A friend of mine had a poodle, and one of its little tricks was to delicately extract a sweet from the lips of its mistress. The guest of honour saw the trick and was greatly impressed. His teeth flashed in the style which caused a million female hearts to beat a little faster. One could almost see little pinpoints of light sparkling from his incisors, canines and molars. Could he try the trick? Of course he could. He was assured that the dog would bite nothing other than the sweet, so he took one between his teeth and offered it to the poodle. With its usual delicacy, the dog grasped the morsel and gently pulled. The sweet stayed put. It bunched its hindquarters and pulled more powerfully. And out popped the sweet — together with a thousand-dollar set of dentures. That was the last time the film star ever tried that trick, I'm sure. The dog worried the sweet free, and the poor chap, looking strangely old and shrunken, retrieved his teeth and beat a hasty retreat to the bathroom.

We all tried not to make too much of the incident, but really we were near to bursting with repressed laughter. I have often pondered on the dreadful consequences if a national newspaper gossip columnist had been present.

Not long after the party, Googie Withers came to see us from her home in Australia where she and her husband, John McCullen, are very popular. She was looking as beautiful as ever, and it was lovely to see her again. Googie immediately asked me if that was my parrot on the roof. We had a hasty check to see if Polly was still on his perch, saw that he was, and then went outside to see a strange parrot sitting comfortably on the roof. It was obviously an escapee so we phoned the police and helped with a full-scale rescue operation. We all made parrot noises, scattered lashings of bird seed around and even brought out Polly to see if he could lure the bird down. But all to no avail. The flyaway was most interested and performed little dances on the roof, but it wouldn't come down. Then we were joined by the anxious owners, who had been contacted by the police.

After a while, the parrot fluttered its wings experimentally, took off, made a circuit of the garden – and then flew away. Everyone was most disappointed.

I'm delighted to say that the story had a happy ending. Twenty-four hours later it flew into someone's kitchen and trapped itself. The police were turned out again, the owners informed, and all parties had a happy reunion. I had promised to phone Googie and tell her of any outcome. She was delighted and said it wasn't everybody who laid on a wild parrot just to make her feel at home.

I always sympathise with Brighton's noted residents because they are for ever being asked to support local causes; one of the penalties of fame, I suppose. However, despite my sympathy, I didn't hesitate to make a personal appeal for help when a local animal rescue service turned to me for some aid. One morning I received a letter from the Worthing Animal Rescue Service. The letter said they were planning a big sponsored walk to try and raise £700 to buy an animal ambulance. How much would I charge to formally start the walk? How much would I charge! I really thought they were joking. I became deeply involved and whipped up a lot of sponsors from my friends, including many of the party guests, plus Kenneth More, Hayley Mills, Olive Gilbert, Anna Massey, Alan Melville, Angela Douglas, Judy Cornwell, Dora Bryan and many others.

Meanwhile, while I was collecting the sponsors, from out of the blue an American woman rang me from the home of old clients with whom she was staying. She introduced herself and said how much she had enjoyed my first book and what was my favourite animal charity? It seemed too good an opportunity to miss, so I told her of the pet rescue organisation and its struggle to raise funds. She promptly sent me a cheque for £100!

It turned out to be a wonderful day. It was a Sunday morning and the weather was glorious as my little party arrived. There was myself, Dorothy, Susan our cook/housekeeper, Ron and, of course, Puddy and Digger Dene who are always ready for a walk.

The route was over the beautiful Sussex Downs, and more than a hundred dogs and their owners surged off as I cut the tape. Ron pushed me for a mile until the path became too rough for a wheelchair, then Dorothy drove me to the halfway stage where everyone, including the dogs, was given refreshments. There was another surprise for the walkers as they straggled in to the finish: a brand new dazzling white ambulance complete with flashing light and radio. There had been so much support for the project that the organisers had been able to buy the vehicle beforehand. And as each owner arrived, they received – with the compliments of Denes – a copy of my book.

It was during this time that a woman with a lively-looking mongrel on a lead came over and said: 'Do you remember us, Mr Lloyd-Jones?' As a matter of fact, I did. Seventeen years previously the owner had brought a puppy to see me which I treated for worms. And here they were again. The dog, despite its advanced age, looked as spry as a two-year-old, and had romped the walk with no trouble.

There was a sequel to this most pleasant day a few months later. The same pet rescue society held a Michaelmas Fair and were astute enough to auction my sponsor cards which bore many famous signatures including the entire cast of Coronation Street. This pulled in another useful sum of money to help the society in its very valuable work.

I would like every sizeable town to have its own ambulance. How can a busy veterinary surgeon in the middle of an operation or a crowded surgery drop everything and go out to rescue an animal hurt in an accident? Doctors can't do it.

I always feel a warm glow when I see animal lovers pulling together in a good cause, but sometimes a person's love for a pet takes a more bizarre form. There was a woman in Brighton who had been a client of mine for many years. She had a toy poodle and she literally lived for the dog. It was a not uncommon relationship between a lonely old woman and her pet, but she was beside herself when the dog finally died at a ripe old age. It was a most harrowing experience to see her grief; she couldn't have been more stricken if she had lost a husband or a child. About six months later, she telephoned and asked me to visit her. I agreed, but I wasn't looking forward to the meeting very much. I was sure in my own mind that she was contemplating buying another dog, and wanted my advice. I sincerely felt that she wasn't a proper person to own another animal because she was so unbalanced and I was wondering how I could tactfully tell her this. Anyway, I turned up at her home in one of Brighton's Regency squares, just off the sea front, and was shown into a rather tatty drawing-room. The first thing I saw was the dog I remembered so well sitting in its usual arm-chair in front of the fire. It had a blue ribbon on its top knot and obviously the woman had just been grooming it – there was a brush, comb and a tin of talcum powder by the chair.

I was really horrified when the truth dawned on me. The woman had had the poor little creature stuffed. Her life still revolved round it and she carried it around everywhere. It even went in her car, occupying its former position on the rear parcel shelf. This is what she had wanted me for – to show me proudly how she had achieved for the dog a pitiful sort of immortality. I felt very sad when I left; the woman was more to be pitied than anything. But then it occurred to me that perhaps she was better in her strange, unbalanced world than starting again with a live dog.

The south coast between Eastbourne and Worthing has more than its share of animal cranks, principally because it has a very high population of elderly people. These poor, usually lonely old people devote themselves to their pets, and one often reads in the local newspapers of an animal giving the alarm and neighbours or police finding its owner dead or incapacitated. It is really very sad. Sociologists call it the 'South Coast Syndrome', where a married couple retire, sell up and leave the surroundings and friends of a lifetime to pursue the dream of a little house on the coast for their retirement. Only too often the dream turns sour. One or other of the partners dies and the survivor drifts into poverty and ill health. It is not surprising that so many of them devote all their affections to their pets.

One such man was Walter. He had an elderly mongrel called Captain, and I treated the dog when Walter's wife was alive. He was absolutely desolate when she died, and became a recluse with only the mongrel for company. I watched the transition with great sadness, for Walter became terrified of anything happening to Captain and brought him to see me with great frequency. On every successive visit the old man looked more seedy and down at heel, and I wondered what he had done with his money, for he used to appear moderately affluent.

About three months had elapsed since his last visit and I began to worry in case anything had happened to him. Then I read a news item in the paper. Apparently neighbours heard feeble barking and alerted the police. They broke in and found that Walter was dead on the bedroom floor and the dog was dreadfully emaciated.

I thought the sequel to the story was even sadder. There was no need for Walter's poverty, because he left quite a lot of money and his home was absolutely stuffed with antique treasures. It had looked like Aladdin's Cave. The old man slept on a Victorian chaise-longue with only a worn old blanket for cover, and he and Captain had been living entirely off tinned soups. And there were more than two hundred clocks in his house, some of them very valuable indeed. What a tragic end to a long life.

The police asked me to look after Captain, and I did so. I eventually found him a home with some friends of mine, and he lived to the ripe old age of seventeen. I must say that Captain's declining years were a good deal happier than his former master's.

It's strange how recluses rarely live entirely alone; most of them cling to the company of one animal or other. A previous owner of Denes Close, where I had my old Brighton practice, had lived a weird life with three enormous alsatians and a butler-cum-oddjob man, who by all accounts was as eccentric

149

as she was. She almost never left the house, and local traders would deliver through a trap door set in the Sussex flint wall. In those days, apparently, it looked like the House of Usher, with the gardens overgrown and a tree growing right through the roof. This tree was later cut down and made into a beam which was used to strengthen the roof it had weakened. I cannot remember the complete circumstances, but the woman and the butler died almost together, and some time elapsed before people heard the howling of the dogs and went to investigate.

It's a familiar story, and a very sad one. It seems awful to me that dogs, which are such wonderful creatures, should so often get saddled with bad owners. It is not a natural life for a dog to share the eccentricities of a recluse. But then, dogs are usually loyal beyond reproach – and cats don't seem to mind.

Another aspect of dog ownership which saddens me is when a person is so fond of a dog that when it dies, he refuses ever to get another animal. It seems to me that if one carries this point of view through to its logical conclusion, one would never get married, have children, or even make any friends in order to avoid the grief of bereavement. It's astonishing how many people react like this.

One person who was dreadfully upset by the death of his dog was Frankie Howerd, that wonderful comedian, whom I met recently at a dinner party. Frankie – he likes to be called Frank off stage – was still very upset at the death of his boxer some time previously. The dog had lived to thirteen, which is a ripe old age for a boxer. He told me the loss had put him off owning another dog and I tried to talk him out of it. It is a great wrench, I know, but life must go on and to some people life just isn't complete without a dog.

It was the first time I had met Frank, although I am a great fan of his on television. I liked him very much indeed. He is a quiet, unassuming and sensitive man, far different from his usual extrovert stage image. I realised then what a superb professional artist he is and what a strain it must be to go out in front of a huge audience and be incomparably funny when really one feels just the opposite.

I know I am a very lucky man in the people I have met, and perhaps it is a fitting disappointment that I had to be content with only a fleeting glimpse of the man I would have most liked to meet – Pope John XXIII, whom Cassandra, the late Daily Mirror columnist, once described as the man who put his arm round the heart of the world.

I was being whisked in the back of a chauffeur-driven Lancia from Rome Airport to Capablo to treat a kennel of pekes, owned by the Marchesa di Bourbon del Monte. I had helped choose a group of pekes for her at Crufts, and they were the start of a glorious kennel which became famous in all the show rings of Europe. We were approaching the port of Civitavecchia when the car was flagged down by a very flustered-looking policeman. We had to halt at some cross-roads, and I was just wondering why the delay, when an enormous limousine came in sight, flanked by police motor cyclists. The whole cortège was travelling at about five miles an hour. In the back of the car, looking for all the world like a mischievous little boy, with a wonderful smile, was His Holiness, Pope John XXIII, the first pontiff to be called by that name since the year 523.

I really can't describe the magic of that smile. It seemed to uplift me spiritually, and I can see it now as clearly as on that hot day on a dusty road in Italy. Like Kennedy, and Churchill, he was a man who caught the imagination of the world but, unlike the two statesmen, there was no one who did not love him.

I read in the papers later that it was his first trip from the Vatican, and an unscheduled trip at that. It caused quite a panic at the time, and he asked the police why. They told him: 'For security reasons.'

'Security?' His Holiness was alleged to have answered. 'Why? I wasn't going to hurt anyone.'

He was on his way to a prison, where he felt he was needed! What a very human man he was.

Chapter Thirteen

A NEW CAREER

The process of applying natural remedies to animals has absorbed me all my life. But things began to crystallise during the war years at the haunted house at Feltham, when human drugs were hard to get and veterinary drugs practically impossible. I was much concerned with finding some sort of substitute for my practice and for the many animals in my care.

Those were the days before penicillin, of course, and there was nothing like the complexity of drugs available as there is now. I was probably the only homeopathic vet practising at the time, and while I naturally preferred traditional remedies like aconite, belladonna, nux vomica and digitalis, I would never hesitate to use conventional drugs in extreme cases. But I found drugs of every kind virtually unobtainable. There was also a feeding problem. The bombed-out and evacuated dogs in my care had to eat, but people had priority over animals and food too was scarce. So it was not surprising that I turned to nature for the answer. I fed the animals as much as possible on home-grown produce. They ate greens, onions and even root vegetables for bulk. It was largely a meatless diet and far from ideal, but they survived. Wartime diets were far from ideal for people, you may remember.

I found that dogs with gastric conditions or worms responded to having garlic added to their meals and, as I have already said, sought it out themselves. I crushed the cloves in my old-fashioned pestle and mortar and experimented with various quantities, carefully studying the results. Often, they were spectacular.

It was a very exciting period of my life. We had a huge clump of elderberry trees in the garden and I used the fruit to treat anaemia, which was a common wartime complaint. Elderberries are a rich source of iron and the prescription worked a treat. I started bottling vast quantities of elderberries so that I could use them throughout the year.

It was about this period when I had a wonderful opportunity

to seek some really expert advice on my work. A client, who was following my theories with great interest, was a friend of Sir Alexander Fleming, that great British scientist who discovered penicillin. He mentioned my work to Sir Alexander, who was then plain mister, with the knighthood and honours yet to come, and a meeting was arranged. We talked for an hour. I found him a kindly, gentle man, much concerned because the medical profession was treating his discovery as a sort of universal cure. He was worried in case it all got out of hand, and in fact his concern was prophetic. It is now known how violently some people react against the drug, and how people have actually died of penicillin poisoning.

But this was all in the future. Sir Alexander was most interested in my theories and very encouraging. He said that pioneer work never came easily and I would have to do a great deal and display much patience before I could develop a new range of natural veterinary medicines. How right he was!

In fact, Sir Alexander discovered his drug way back in 1929, and it was not developed for medicinal use until World War II. But the great man told me that he may well have been anticipated by 4,000 years. Apparently, there is evidence to suggest that the Egyptians of 2000 BC treated wounds successfully with a certain type of fungus. Was it a type of penicillin? If not, it was very similar. Mother Nature again.

During the rest of the war I continued experimenting, drawing up careful tables of ingredients, quantities and the results. It was all very promising and when peace came I began to think I was really getting somewhere: It was the birth of Denes Veterinary Herbal Products, although the future of the infant was still obscure. My first step was to approach a well known firm of herbalists in London and ask them whether it was possible to make powders and pills from extracts from natural sources. We had several lengthy discussions based on a list of ingredients; and finally they said yes. The first products made to my prescriptions were garlic pills, seaweed powder, elderberry pills, my old favourite, and greenleaf pills, which were made from the chlorophyll extracted from the leaves of various wild plants and herbs.

There were, of course, other problems. The biggest was obtaining sufficient quantities of the raw materials to allow bulk manufacture to go ahead. The manufacturer handled the problems of supply by organising freelance collectors up and down the country. If any of them had appeared on the What's My Line game, I reckon they would have beaten the panel hands down.

Later, when things became much bigger, we had to find other sources. Nowadays, Denes suppliers are all over the world. Most of the garlic, for instance, comes from France. Tree bark is grown in South America, and the seaweed comes from Northern Ireland, where in some districts it is a valuable human food served rather like a vegetable. However, the parsley and watercress are British.

Another problem concerned the manufacturing process itself. Expensive machinery had to be installed to turn elderberries into pills, etc, and naturally the makers wanted a guarantee that there would be sufficient business for them to justify a large capital expenditure. I gulped, and said yes. But this assurance worried me a lot, because the company still wasn't off the ground, and I was taking on a considerable responsibility without really knowing anything of the commercial implications. But in for a penny, in for a pound. I gradually added to the range and more problems of manufacture had to be solved. Things like raspberry and rhubarb were developed and processed for their marvellous curative properties.

It was all very exciting, but the strain was beginning to tell and I was badly in need of a holiday. So I went off to Spain, staying in a marvellous village on the coast near Barcelona. In those days the country was almost completely undiscovered and there wasn't a package-deal tourist in sight. I suppose that was the reason why everything was very inexpensive and wonderfully unspoiled, although the standard of living for the average person was pretty awful.

Overlooking the village was a range of dramatic, startlingly white cliffs with hordes of workmen toiling patiently every day digging out chalk and loading it into lorries. I assumed it was just chalk and nothing more, and thought no more about it until I became friendly with the local vet. He spoke very good English and obviously we had a lot in common, so there was much to talk about. One day I mentioned the chalk and he told me it had a curious mineral content and was also slightly radioactive. It was used as a regional medicinal remedy and was excellent for all types of gastric conditions. My ears pricked up at this. 'Tell me,' I said, 'have you ever used it for animals?' He had, and with splendid results. He got hold of a big bag of the stuff and I took it back home with me. I remember declaring eight pounds of chalk at the customs, and some of the strange looks I received! They examined it closely and did everything except run a geiger counter over it – which, under the circumstances, was a very good thing! I think they thought I was a drug smuggler.

I tried the chalk on animals with gastric troubles and the results were excellent. It took me several months to arrive at the right quantity for various animals, and when I ran out of my original supply, I eventually arranged to import the magic chalk. It proved a valuable addition to the Denes range of products and I used it quite a lot in my work.

This story had a strange sequel. As I said earlier, it was used in Spain as a regional remedy, but gradually its fame spread and it became famous all over Spain and later in France and Germany too. But the supplies were not endless and the people became worried about conservation. So the supply dried up so far as Denes was concerned and I had reluctantly to drop the chalk from my natural armoury.

At this stage, Denes was not in being as a limited company. I was using the bulk of the products for my own practice, which in those days was growing rapidly. I would prescribe clients packets of one thing or another for their pets, but things became a little awkward as the word got round, and I was being asked for vast quantities for whole kennels of eighty to a hundred dogs. The demand was all very encouraging, but it was soon obvious that the only sensible way to really establish my brainchild was to form a company and market the products properly. But here was a snag. Because I was on the register of practising vets, I was not allowed to have any financial or commercial interests in anything allied to my profession. This is a most sensible rule and I would not have dreamed of trying to get round it. So I was in something of a dilemma. On one hand there was a move obvious to any businessman (which I am not) and on the other was a constraint imposed by my profession.

I overcame the difficulties by having two friends, Hal Higgs and another, form the company. My only interests in the company were acting in an advisory capacity and in the development of new products. I religiously observed the rules of my profession and never took so much as a penny from Denes while I was on the register of practising vets.

The company was formed for two reasons. Firstly, as the only outlet I could not generate sufficient quantities of the products to justify the high initial cost of manufacture. Secondly, I sincerely wanted to pass on the boon of natural health for pets to a far larger section of the public than I could possibly reach on my own.

Business jogged along for several years, and the products gained a splendid reputation both in England and on the Continent without making the two principals a lot of money. For years I was Denes' best customer, buying the products for my own practice. *All* I received in the way of perks was the normal trade discount – something which applied to anybody who was purchasing in the quantity that I was.

Denes was run by Hal Higgs but his health started fading sadly. This is where Eric Sawyer came on the scene and took over as managing director.

I first met Eric and his charming wife Mary many years ago when they brought their dogs to my London surgery, and at a later date I was able to assist them when they started breeding alsatians. They also took in sick animals, calling on me to treat them. We worked together then quite closely, and I, in turn, often recommended his kennels as I knew they were run very well.

We continued our friendship over the years. Then while I was at Midhurst – I must sound like a fixture there! – Eric and Mary, who lived nearby, came to see me. I suppose I must have been feeling pretty depressed because I poured out my troubles and told them Denes was rapidly running out of executives due to ill health. Much to my astonishment, Eric told me he had just sold his business to an American company and that he was looking for something else to do, because he was much too young to retire to a rocking-chair on the porch.

Then he offered to step in and re-establish Denes on a sound business footing. Naturally, I was delighted. Eric was the ideal man for the job. He combined a genuine feeling for animals with considerable business acumen and he was a believer in my methods. He rolled up his sleeves and started work with characteristic energy.

It didn't take him long to establish the company on a sound basis. And then, to my inexpressible delight, he asked me to take an active part in the business.

Life follows some curious paths, but this for me was the most unexpected one of all. Years ago, when my outlook looked very bleak and depressing, a healer told me that one day I would work with animals again. I would have given anything to have believed him. Denes moved to Brighton and started selling through retail shops.

Now I frequently answer letters about every aspect of animal ownership. Of course I miss the practical side of a veterinary practice and regrettably won't ever be able to manage it again.

However it is good to be able to be of some help with animals again.

Famous Animal Books in Fontana

Joy Adamson
The Spotted Sphinx (*Illus.*) *40p*
Born Free (*Illus.*) *35p*
Living Free (*Illus.*) *35p*
Forever Free (*Illus.*) *40p*

George Adamson
Bwana Game (*Illus.*) *40p*

Gerald Durrell
Birds, Beasts and Relatives *30p*
Two in the Bush *30p*
Rosy is My Relative *30p*

Jacquie Durrell
Beasts in My Bed (*Illus.*) *30p*

Virginia McKenna
Some of My Friends Have Tails (*Illus.*) *25p*

Bernard and Michael Grzimek
Serengeti Shall Not Die (*Illus.*) *45p*

Buster Lloyd-Jones
The Animals Came in One by One *25p*

Harry Wolhuter
Memories of a Game Ranger *40p*

 Fontana Books

Fontana Modern Novels

The Once and Future King T. H. White *60p*
'A magnificent and tragic tapestry . . . irresistible.'
Sunday Times

The Tin Men Michael Frayn *30p*
'Goes straight into the Evelyn Waugh class.' *Sunday Times*

The Invisible Man H. G. Wells *30p*
The classic masterpiece of a scientist trapped by his own discovery.

Anthony Powell

A Question of Upbringing *30p*

A Buyer's Market *30p*

The Acceptance World *35p*

At Lady Molly's *30p*

Casanova's Chinese Restaurant *35p*

The Kindly Ones *35p*

The Soldier's Art *30p*

The Military Philosophers *35p*

Books Do Furnish a Room *35p*

'His magnificent series *A Dance to the Music of Time.*'
Evening Standard

 Fontana Modern Novels

Fontana Books

Fontana is best known as one of the leading paperback publishers of popular fiction and non-fiction. It also includes an outstanding, and expanding section of books on history, natural history, religion and social sciences.

Most of the fiction authors need no introduction. They include Agatha Christie, Hammond Innes, Alistair MacLean, Catherine Gaskin, Victoria Holt and Lucy Walker. Desmond Bagley and Maureen Peters are among the relative newcomers.

The non-fiction list features a superb collection of animal books by such favourites as Gerald Durrell and Joy Adamson.

All Fontana books are available at your bookshop or news-agent; or can be ordered direct. Just fill in the form below and list the titles you want.

————————————————————————————

FONTANA BOOKS, Cash Sales Department, P.O. Box 4, Godalming, Surrey. Please send purchase price plus 5p postage per book by cheque, postal or money order. No currency.

NAME (Block letters)

_____

ADDRESS

_____

_____

_____